A COMPANION TO TEACHING OF ENGLISH

A COMPANION TO TEACHING OF ENGLISH

B. SALIM

ATLANTIC
PUBLISHERS & DISTRIBUTORS (P) LTD

Published by

ATLANTIC

PUBLISHERS & DISTRIBUTORS (P) LTD

7/22, Ansari Road, Darya Ganj,
New Delhi-110002
Phones : +91-11-40775252, 23273880, 23275880, 23280451
Fax : +91-11-23285873
Web : www.atlanticbooks.com
E-mail : orders@atlanticbooks.com

Branch Office
5, Nallathambi Street, Wallajah Road,
Chennai-600002
Phones : +91-44-64611085, 32413319
E-mail : chennai@atlanticbooks.com

Printed in India at Nice Printing Press, A-33/3A, Site-IV, Industrial Area, Sahibabad, Ghaziabad, U.P.

PREFACE

The book, *A Companion to Teaching of English,* aims at enabling the M.A. students in answering essay questions, paragraph questions, short questions-answers and comprehension questions based on the teaching of English. The first chapter traces the questions of language and language related issues in the ELT context. The second chapter is about the position of the English language in the world of today and SLA theories. The third chapter probes into linguistics and language teaching. The fourth chapter is a glance at the striking linguistic dichotomies. The fifth chapter sums up the different methods and approaches of teaching English. The last chapter is devoted to discuss teaching of English. A glossary of ELT terms is presented. I do not make any authentic claims in preparing this companion. Views, reviews and suggestions, if any, for improving the book in the next edition are welcome.

B. SALIM

CONTENTS

1

Language

The question 'What is language?' is comparable with 'What is life?' Everybody knows what life is but one cannot present a satisfactory definition of life. The same is the case with language. The term 'language' can be understood better in terms of its characteristics. Linguists define language in their own ways.

Robins rightly points out that definitions tend to be trivial and uninformative. But he does list and discuss a number of salient facts that must be taken into account in any seriously intended study of language. He views : "Language is a symbol system based on pure arbitrary conventions....infinitely extendable and modifiable according to the changing needs and conditions of the speakers." Every language selects some symbols from the alphabet of the language and joins in different combinations to form meaningful words. The system is purely arbitrary in the sense that there is no one to one correspondence between the structure of a word and the thing it stands. Language conventions are not easily changed yet it is not impossible to do so. Language is infinitely extendable and modifiable. Words go on changing meanings. New words continue to be added to language.

According to Edward Sapir, "Language is purely human and non-instinctive method of communicating ideas, emotions and desires by means of a system of voluntarily produced symbols." Sapir has rightly said that language is human. Only humans possess language. Animals do have a communication system but it is not a developed system. That is why language is said to be species-specific and species-uniform. Also, language does not pass from a parent to a child. In this sense it is non-instinctive. A child has to learn language. He/she learns the language of the society he/she is placed in. Sapir's definition suffers from several defects. However broadly we construe the terms 'idea,' 'emotion' and 'desire,' there is much that is communicated by language which is not covered by them.

In his *Essay on Language* Hall tells us that "Language is the institution whereby humans communicate and interact with one another by means of habitually used oral auditory arbitrary symbols." This definition rightly gives more prominence to the fact that language is primarily speech produced by oral-auditory symbols. A speaker produces some string of oral sounds that get conveyed through the air to the speaker who receives the sound waves and conveys these to the brain that interprets these symbols to arrive at a meaning. Hall, like Sapir, treats language as a purely human institution.

In their *Outline of Linguistic Analysis* Block and Trager wrote : "A language is a system of arbitrary vocal symbols by means of which a social group co-operates." This definition makes no appeal to the communicative function of language. It stresses the social function.

Noam Chomsky in *Syntactic Structures* defines : "A language is a set (finite or infinite) of sentences, each finite in length and constructed out of a finite set of elements." It says nothing about the communicative function. Its purpose is to focus attention upon the purely structural properties of languages.

Darbyshire said : "Language is undoubtedly a kind of means of communication among human beings. It consists primarily of vocal sounds. It is articulatory, systematic and arbitrary." Before the start of civilization man might have used the language of signs but it must have had a very limited scope. Language is a fully developed means of communication with the civilized man who can convey and receive millions of messages across the world. An entire civilization depends on language only. Language has changed the entire gamut of human relations and made it possible for human beings to grow into a human community on this planet.

Language is a system of conventional spoken or written symbols by means of which human beings, as members of a social group and participants in its culture, communicate — Encyclopaedia Britannica.

It follows that the definitions are not satisfactory. It would be better to list out the characteristics of language and discuss them in detail.

Characteristics

Language is a very important means of communication. It is very difficult to think of a society without language. It sharpens and sharpens people's thoughts and guides and controls their entire activity. It is a carrier of civilization and culture. It is present everywhere in all activities. It is as important as the air we breathe. It is the most valuable possession of man. In the scheme of things all humans are blessed with language. It is the specific property of the humans. Humans are talking animals. They can send an infinite number of messages to their fellow beings. It is through language that they store knowledge, transfer it to the next generation and yoke the present, past and the future together.

Language is arbitrary. Had language not been arbitrary, there would have been only one language in the world. The arbitrary nature of language permits change but such changes do not normally take place. Names once given are not normally changed. Words in a language are more difficult to change because a whole society has accepted them.

Language is a system of systems. Language is not an amorphous, a disorganised or chaotic combination of sounds. Sounds are arranged in certain fixed or established systematic order to form meaningful units or words. Similarly, words are also arranged in a particular system to frame acceptable meaningful sentences. These systems operate at two levels — phonological and syntactical. At the phonological level sounds of a language appear only in some fixed combinations. There is no word, for example, that starts with bz-, lr-, or zl- combination. Again, there are several English words having an initial consonant cluster with three consonants (*e.g.*, string, spring). But there is no tetraphonic consonant cluster (a string of four consonants in the same syllable). There is no word that begins with /j/ or ends with /h/. Similarly, words too combine to form sentences according to some certain grammatical or structural rules.

Language is primarily made up of vocal sounds only produced by a physiological articulatory mechanism in the human body. Writing must have come much later as an intelligent attempt to represent vocal sounds. Writing is only the graphic representation of the sounds of the language. Writing did have an advantage over speech — it could be preserved in books or records. It has lost that advantage too. The age-old proverb 'pen is mightier than the sword' does not hold much ground.

Language differs from animal communication. Language makes use of clearly distinguishable discrete, separately indentifiable symbols. Animal communications are closed systems that permit of no change, modification or addition. Language is changing, growing everyday, and new words continue to be added. Human language is far more structurally complex than animal communication. English, for example, has 44 sounds that join in different groups to form thousands of words. These words can be arranged into millions of sets to frame different sentences. Each sentence has its own internal structure. There is no such structural complexity in a lamb's bleating or a monkey's cry. The process of learning plays an important part in the acquisition of language. An important property possessed by human language is displacement. A human being can talk about the past, the present, or the future, of an event that happened nearby or thousands of miles away. An animal cannot do it. When a dog produces a certain sound, it generally refers to the present. This property of displacement enables the humans to create fiction and describe the past as well as the possible future events.

Language is a form of social behaviour. Language has to be learnt. This learning is possible only in society.

Language is a symbol system. A symbol is a concrete event, object or mark that stands for something relatively abstract. A cross, for example, is a symbol that stands for the great sacrifice of Jesus Christ, his crucifixion on the cross, besides being symbol of a Christian. Similarly, words are also symbols that stand for objects.

Language is an inseparable part of human society. It is through language that humanity has come out of the stone age and has developed.

Language Acquisition

Language acquisition is the process by which a child acquires its mother tongue. The acquisition of a first language is the most wonderful feat we perform in our whole life, and we do it at an age when we can hardly do anything else.

The serious linguistic investigation of acquisition dates mainly from the 1940s, when the Roman linguist Roman Jakobson published a pioneering study. In 1957 the American psychologist B.F. Skinner published *Verbal Behaviour,* an attempt at explaining acquisition within the framework of behaviourism. This book was savagely reviewed by the American linguist Noam Chomsky. From about 1960s intensive studies of children acquiring their first language became increasingly frequent. We now know a great deal about what children can be observed to do as they acquire their first language. Language acquisition is an active process. Children take the clues available to them and use these clues to construct their own grammatical rules, rules which grow in sophistication as acquisition proceeds.

Language Acquisition Device

Language Acquisition Device (LAD) is a hypothetical mental organ dedicated to the acquisition of a first language. In the 1960s Noam Chomsky began developing his innateness hypothesis by which we are born already knowing what human languages are like. Chomsky elaborated his hypothesis by arguing that children must possess a language acquisition device, a specific mental organ, a structure in the brain which is dedicated to extracting from haphazard and often degenerate speech the generalizations required for the child to construct the necessary rules of phonology and grammar. The LAD is purely hypothetical. No one has yet identified any areas or structures in the brain which seem to have the required characteristics. Many critics see the LAD as a fantasy. Chomsky himself has seemingly abandoned his claims for the LAD in favour of an even stronger claim. He now believes that so much information about the nature of human language is already present in our brains at birth that all a child has to do is to 'set a few switches' to the correct values for the language being acquired. This is his parameter-setting model.

Language and Ethnicity

Language and ethnicity refers to the relation between language use and ethnic background, especially in a mixed community. In modern urban societies, it is now common place to find speakers of a variety of ethnic backgrounds living together and interacting in various ways. Examples included Angos, Latinos and blacks in western American cities and speakers of Anglo-Saxon, Caribbean and Asian origin in English cities. Especially since the 1980s, some linguists have begun turning their attention to the links between language and ethnic background. The study of language and ethnicity is sometimes called ethno linguistics.

Language and Identity

Language and identity refers to the role of language in providing a speaker with individuality and group membership. Everytime you open your mouth, you give other people important clues about what sort of person you are, where you come from, what social class you belong to, even your sex and age (for example on the phone). This information says something both about your individuality and about the social, national and ethnic groups to which you consider yourself to belong. Socio-linguists have realized that providing each speaker with an individual and group identity is one of the most important functions of language.

Language and Ideology

A language can be used as an instrument of social pressure. Language can be used either to confer validity upon a social group or political entity or to deny validity. For example, after the French Revolution the new Republican government resolved to unify the country. Laws were passed requiring the teaching and use of Parisian French, while the other languages were subjected to merciless condemnation and persecution, their use was presented as unpatriotic, subversive and sinister; their speakers were condemned as reactionaries and fanatics. The political and ideological uses of language have been examined for generations.

Language and Power

The link between language and power is very striking. In almost every society of any size or complexity there are notable differences in the type of language used by different sectors of society. For example, in the English speaking world, the contrast is primarily between standard English and the various non-standard forms of English. It is obvious that speakers of standard English typically enjoy more power, more prestige and more money than the others who are far more likely to be confined to positions of low prestige with comparatively little money or influence.

Language Areas

The regions of the brain which are devoted to particular aspects of the use of language are marked as language areas. The French surgeon Paul Broca and the German neurologist Carl Wernicke identified two well-defined areas in the brain which play a crucial role in the use of language. Both are located in the left hemisphere of the cerebral cortex, the wrinkly grey outer layer of the brain, in the vast majority of people. Wernicke's area is located behind and above the ear. It is responsible for comprehension and also for access to ordinary vocabulary in speaking. Broca's area is located close to the temple. It is responsible for providing the necessary grammatical structure. In speech, it also controls intonation and the fine muscular movements of the speech organs. During listening, speech signals are passed by the ears to the auditory part of the brain which processes the sounds and sends the result to Wernicke's area for interpretation. During speech, Wernicke's area provides the ordinary vocabulary to Broca's area which embeds this vocabulary into the required grammatical structure and then sends its instructions to the organs of speech. With a high degree of reliability, damage to any of these areas produces the expected language disability.

Language Change

One of the fundamental facts about living languages is that they are always changing. New words, new pronunciations, new grammatical forms and structures, and new meanings for existing words are always coming into existence, while older ones are always dropping out of use. It is absolutely impossible for a living language to avoid changing. The motivation for change are many and various. New objects, new concepts, new activities all require new names. At the same time old objects and activities may cease to exist, and their names may die with them. Certain linguistic forms may acquire social prestige. The physiological characteristics of the mouth may tend to favour certain changes in pronunciation. Such changes may disrupt formerly regular grammatical patterns. Syntactic structures which come to be frequently used may be reduced to simpler grammatical forms. And language contact may induce speakers to import forms and usages from other languages. Such constant change means that a language at any point in time is always significantly different from its direct ancestor of some centuries earlier. A language spoken over a sizeable area does not change everywhere in the same way.

Language Contact

The speakers of any given language are almost always in some kind of contact with the speakers of one or more other languages. When two different languages are spoken in adjacent areas, speakers on both sides of the boundary will be exposed to the other language, and may often gain some fluency in that other language. Because of conquest or migration, speakers of two or more languages may be mixed together in a single community. Speakers of one language may travel and become exposed to different languages spoken elsewhere. In modern times the mass media have brought awareness of a number of languages into regions in which these were formerly unknown. The consequences of contact may range from the trivial to the far-reaching. Speakers may merely take over a few words from their neighbours. This is called borrowing. The words borrowed are loan words in the receiving language. Language contacts affect grammar and pronunciation.

Language Death

Language death means the disappearance of a language as a mother tongue. A language comes under enormous pressure from a more prestigious or more widely used language spoken nearby. Native speakers of the language under pressure may find themselves obliged to use it in an ever-greater number of contexts. Eventually, a time may come when many children are no longer learning the threatened language as their mother tongue, or are learning it only imperfectly. At this point we say the threatened language is moribund or dying. The inevitable result is that within a generation or two, no one will be able to speak the threatened language at all. This is language death. The process which leads to it is language shift. Language death is usually gradual. The language may disappear completely from some area while surviving in others. The final outcome is a dead language.

Language Disability

Language disabilities refer to any pathological condition which has adverse consequences for the sufferer's ability to use language. Language disabilities must be carefully distinguished from speech defects like stuttering, lisping and stammering. A true disability results either from a genetic defect or from damage to the language areas in the brain. Since the possible types of damage and defects are virtually limitless, individual sufferers naturally exhibit an enormous range of disabilities. We hardly ever find two individuals with exactly the same symptoms. The best known disabilities are the several types of aphasia. But other types exist. For example, Williams syndrome is known to result from a genetic defect in chromosome number eleven. But the known range of disabilities is positively startling. A bilingual sufferer may lose one language completely but retain the second perfectly, and then, after sometime, may lose the second but regain the first. Many types of disability are characterized by greater or lesser degrees of anomia, the inability to remember words for things. Some sufferers have the inability to use or understand words denoting fruits and vegetables, with no other problem at all. Some people lose verbs but retain nouns.

Language Faculty

Language faculty is our biological ability to use language. Human beings are the only creatures on earth that use language. Our language faculty is real. It is largely distinct from all of our other cognitive abilities. Chomsky and others have long argued that our language faculty must consist of a number of specialized and largely independent subcomponents which interact in specific ways to produce our overall linguistic behaviour. More recently, some people have begun to question whether our language faculty as a whole should itself be regarded as a distinctive part of our mental equipment. The study of all the biological aspects of our language faculty is sometimes called biolinguistics.

Language Family

Every living language is constantly changing. The changes which affect the language in one place do not necessarily affect it in other places. Consequently, if the language is spoken over any significant area, it will tend to break up into rather distinct varieties. At first these are merely the regional dialects of the language. Given sufficient time, they may become so different from one another that we are forced to regard them as separate languages; the daughter languages of that single ancestral language or mother tongue. The daughter languages may in turn break up into further daughter languages. All the languages that share a common ancestor constitute a single language family. Around 300 such language families have been identified by linguists.

Language Instinct

Language instinct is the powerful tendency of children to acquire language. Any physically normal child who is adequately exposed to a language will learn it perfectly. A child exposed to two or three languages will learn all of them. A hearing child normally learns the surrounding spoken language. A deaf child exposed to a sign language will learn that. Children exposed only to a pidgin will turn that pidgin into a real language — a creole. A group of children exposed to no language at all will invent their own and use it. For a long time linguists were slow to appreciate the significance of these observations. From about the 1970s the examination of these phenomena convinced almost all working linguists. We now realize that children are born with a powerful biological drive to learn language. In the 1990s the Canadian psycholinguist Steven Pinker coined, the felicitous term 'language instinct' to denote this remarkable aspect of our biological endowment.

Language in Use

With the decline of the traditional but often deadly dull grammar-and-parsing approach to the study of language in English speaking schools in the 1960s, educators cast about for a new and more engaging technique to replace it. One solution which emerged in 1970s, most notably in Britain, was the language-in-use approach. It focuses upon the varied uses of language in real situations. The aim of this method is to present pupils with real and meaningful examples of English, both spoken and written. This approach has proved to be able to capture the interest of pupils.

Language Myths

Language myths refer to the widely held but false beliefs about individual languages or about language in general. Linguists as recent and eminent as Otto Jesperson have maintained that some languages spoken today are 'primitive' or 'savage' languages, characterized by strange grammatical systems supposedly reflecting a primordial human view of the world. The fact is that every human language ever discovered has a rich and complex grammar and a vocabulary of many thousands of words.

Language Planning

Very commonly, a language 'just grows.' It develops and changes in response to countless small decisions made more or less unconsciously by its speakers. But it is perfectly possible for the future of a language to be determined in important respects by deliberate, self-conscious decisions, often made on an official basis. This is language planning — making deliberate decisions about the form of a language. Sometimes it is called linguistic engineering.

Language Processing

Whenever we produce in utterance, or whenever we hear and understand one, there is a great deal of elaborate activity going on in our brain. This activity is language processing. Psycholinguists have developed a battery of techniques for working out the stages involved in language processing.

Lexicon

Lexicon refers to the vocabulary of a language. Every speaker of a language possesses a certain vocabulary. This may be divided into one's active vocabulary and passive vocabulary. In linguistics we use the term lexicon to the total store of words available to speakers.

Lingua-franca

Lingua-franca is a term for a language which is widely used in some region for communication among people speaking a variety of languages. The original lingua-franca was a variety of Italian, strongly laced with words from French, Spanish, Greek, Arabic and Turkish used as a trade language in the eastern Mediterranean during the late Middle Ages. Since then the term is applied to any language which enjoys wide use among speakers of a variety of different languages in some region.

Linguistic Area

Linguistic area refers to a geographical region in which several unrelated or distantly related languages have striking characteristics in common. With only a very few exceptions, speakers of a language are always in contact with neighbours speaking different languages. The resulting language contact means that words, speech sounds and even grammatical forms may pass from some languages into neighbouring languages. As a result a number of striking characteristics diffuse throughout a geographical region, becoming prominent in a number of languages which are unrelated. Several linguistic areas have been identified by linguists. South East Asia is a striking case. There are many languages including Burmese, Thai and Vietnamese. The study of language area is called areal linguistics.

Metalanguage

Metalanguage is a language used to talk about another language. Linguists, philosophers and many others often need to talk about particular languages or about languages in general. Naturally the discussion itself should be couched in a language of some sort. We must distinguish between the object language and the metalangauge. English can be a metalanguage to talk about English. If we fail to distinguish between the English we are talking about and the English we are using to talk about, we can easily become lost. When we use English as a metalanguage to talk about languages, we need to invoke, a battery of technical terms and concepts, just as a specialist studying physics, music or psychology needs to invoke technical terms and concepts.

Sign Language

Sign language is a language whose medium is signs made with the hands and head. Deaf people cannot hear speech, and many deaf people learn and use a sign language as their primary language, often as their first language. Many different sign languages exist including British Sign Language (BSL) in the UK and American Sign Language (ASL) in the USA. These two are not related to each other, and neither is related in any way to English. A true sign language is not a crude approximation to a spoken language. It is a genuine natural language with a large vocabulary and a rich and complex grammar. It is as flexible and expressive as a spoken language. Since the pioneering work of American linguist Ursula Bellugi in the 1970s sign languages have come to be treated on a par with spoken languages.

Standard Language

Standard language is that variety of a language considered by its speakers to be most appropriate in formal and educational contexts. Consider the case of English. English is spoken as a mother tongue by some 400 million people, as an everyday second language by tens of millions more, and a fluent foreign language by further millions. Many of these people also write in English. The English used by all these people is far from uniform. There are regional differences and differences among social groups. Today socio-linguists speak of English to denote the whole range of varieties. One of these varieties has a special status. This variety is called Standard English. Standard English is the form of English acquired through education. Acquisition of standard English is a large part of what we understand as education in the English speaking world. Most broadcasting and almost all publication is couched in Standard English. In recent years there has been a serious debate among academics and educators about the place of Standard English in education.

Sexist Language

Sexist Language is language which, deliberately or unconsciously, is patronizing or contemptuous towards one sex, usually women. Sexism is not specifically a linguistic issue. But it shows up in languages in various ways. As is well-known, English has only the sex-marked singular pronouns 'he' and 'she.' Hence, a speaker addressing or talking about a mixed group has a problem. 'Somebody has forgotten his umbrella' is sexist, while 'somebody has forgotten his or her umbrella' is clumsy. In popular speech this problem can be solved by using 'their' : 'Somebody has forgotten their umbrella.' But this does not work always. Many pairs of sex-marked words have developed very differently. A 'master' is a powerful or skilful man; a 'mistress' is a woman kept for sexual purposes. A 'courtier' is a polished man of high social status; a 'courtesan' is just an up-market whore. There is nothing wrong with calling a man a 'bachelor,' but calling a woman a 'spinster' is contemptuous. Even a single word may behave differently. In American English, when you call a man a 'pro,' you mean that he is experienced, competent and reliable. When you call a woman a 'pro' you mean she is a prostitute. Sexist language has been drawing the fire of feminists for several decades now. A number of linguists have turned their attention to this issue.

Pidgin

Pidgin is an auxiliary language created by people with no language in common. Very many times in human history, people with no language in common have found themselves thrown together and obliged to deal with one another. Sometimes the language of just one group will be learned by the others and used as a lingua-franca, often something different happens. Words from one or more of the languages of the people involved will be taken and stitched together into a kind of crude way of communicating. This is a pidgin. A pidgin is nobody's mother tongue. It is not a real language at all. It has no recognizable grammar. It is very limited in what it can convey. Different people will speak it differently. Pidgins can and do arise whenever the conditions are favourable, and very many have been created just in the last few hundred years. There are several possible fates for a pidgin. It may eventually drop out of use. The Hawaiian pidgin is now displaced by English. The pidgin can remain in use for generations as has happened with some west African pidgins. A pidgin can be turned into a mother tongue. This happens when the children in a community have nothing but a pidgin to use with other children. The children take the pidgin and turn it into a real language by fixing and elaborating the grammar and expanding the vocabulary. The result is a creole. The children who create it are the first native speakers of the creole. The process of turning a pidgin into a creole is creolization. Countless creoles have come into existence, often because of the activities of European colonists.

Slang

We all use our language in different ways, depending on the circumstances. We speak differently in formal contexts and in informal contexts. Especially when speaking informally, we often take pleasure in resorting to slang informal but colourful words and expressions. Slang expressions are usually introduced by the members of a particular social group. They may remain the property of that group and serve as a badge of group identity, or they may become much more widely known and used. The majority of slang forms are transient. Slang has been described as 'language at play.' The best slang is colourful, exuberant, witty and memorable.

Stylistics

Stylistics is the study of the aesthetic uses of languages, particularly the use of language in literature. The European linguistic tradition has almost always seen the study of the purely structural aspects of language as bound up with the study of its aesthetic aspects. The great Russian linguist Roman Jakobson contributed to theoretical linguistics and to the critical examination of literary works. In the English speaking world a number of scholars have been applying the analytical techniques of theoretical linguistics to the elucidation of literary works and to the examination of the aesthetic aspects of language generally.

A practitioner of stylistics may choose to pursue such topics as the ironic use of language in the novels of V.S. Naipaul, the sound structure of a poem by Dylan Thomas, and so on. In stylistics there is the explicit use of the concepts and analytical techniques of linguistic theory.

Semiotics

Semiotics is the study of the social production of meaning from sign systems. Semiotics, also called semiology, traces its origins to the work of Ferdinand de Saussure, particularly to his idea of the linguistic sign. Semiotics has never been regarded as part of linguistics. It has been developed almost exclusively by non-linguists, particularly in France. In the English-speaking world it enjoys almost no institutional recognition.

Variation

Variation is the existence of observable differences in the way a language is used in a speech community. It is common place observation that a single language is not used in a totally homogeneous manner within a single community. Men do not speak like women. Older people do not speak like younger people. Even the speech of a single person is not homogeneous. This variation was long regarded by linguists as no more than a collection of tiresome data getting in the way of good descriptions, as something to be swept under the carpet and forgotten about. But times have changed. In the 1960s the sociolonguists led by the American William Labov began to make variation a central object of investigation. The result has been a revolution in linguistics. Variation is a vital part of ordinary linguistic behaviour. Variation often shows strong correlations with social variables like social class and sex. The concept of a sociolinguistic variable has become central to the description of speech. It has been discovered that variation is typically the vehicle of language change.

Individual Variation in Language Learning

Learning a language requires the operation of an innate capacity possessed by all human beings. Success in learning a foreign language through instruction will vary from individual to individual, and from group to group. With varying degrees of convictions many explanations are offered for the lack of success of a poor learner. Perhaps, his not 'gifted for language,' or whereas he has a visual memory the method of teaching which is purely oral. Possibly, his 'musical ear' is poor so that he cannot reproduce the sounds of the foreign language. Alternatively, he may be better suited to learning 'analytically.' His failure to use the spoken language with any ease may be due to an introverted personality. He is 'not well-motivated.' The older he is, the more likely it is that his age will be put forward as the explanation of his failure to learn.

The converse of any of these statements may account for the success of the rapid learner. The explanations are offered from experience and subjective assessment of the relevant factors. D.A. Wilkins probes into three factors which are thought to underlie individual variation in Language learning : language aptitude, motivation and age.

Language Aptitude

People are not identical in their capacity for learning a foreign language. We expect some people to learn a language better than others. Whether their language learning potential is the product of innate abilities or the result of their previous learning experience does not matter. We suppose that neither influence can be reversed and that each individual possesses a stable and permanent ability to which we give the name 'language aptitude.'

Research into language aptitude has been carried out to construct tests that provide a reliable prediction of a pupil's success in learning a language. There are two existing aptitude tests : Carroll and Sapon's Modern Language Aptitude Test and Pinsleur's Language Aptitude Battery. The MLAT consists entirely of tests that require the manipulation of language. The LAB has both linguistic and non-linguistic elements.

Motivation

Motivation is a term which occurs in discussion of second rather than first language learning. It is through speech that a child learns to organize his perception and regulate his behaviour and mental activities. Faced with problems and needs, the child will, in his early years, merely look for outside assistance. Language will have the function for him of obtaining this assistance. There will come a stage during which the child learns talking to himself or to anyone who cares to listen to find solution to his needs. Finally the external speech is internalized. The child's behaviour is no longer simply a response to external stimuli. He has come under the control of his thought processes. It is the environment that is controlled by the child.

The parallel between this and the situation in which the second language learner finds himself is limited. The learner does not need the language in order to regulate his behaviour and his mental processes or to organize his perception. When he comes to learn a new language, his modes of behaviour are already set in the ways that are appropriate to his first language culture. Of the child learning his mother-tongue, it could be said that he has the best of all possible motives for learning the language. It enables him to get what he wants. With his increasing proficiency he can obtain more and more complex responses from the people around him. The responses may be verbal or physical. The child learns to influence the behaviour of others in ways that suit him. The same conditions may arise in an alternate language learning situation.

If to influence the actions and thoughts of others, to pursue our occupation and our recreation, it is necessary to use a foreign language, we will learn that foreign language more rapidly and effectively. If we may call this environmental pressure to learn a form of motivation, then we would expect it to operate mostly among immigrants. Not all new residents in a country will learn the language of the host community by any means. If they are members of a sizeable group still speaking the mother-tongue, they will learn the target language correspondingly less well. Those who work in the host community will learn better than those who stay in the home. The children will learn best of all because language will have the greatest value for them.

This kind of motivation is inevitably, characteristic of language 'learning' situation but not of language teaching situation. It is in 'natural' learning situations that the individual is under pressure to acquire the language to control the behaviour of others. Where a foreign language is being learned in the pupil's mother-tongue country, this pressure does not exist.

The need to use the language may be created by directing the pupil's attention not at the language itself but at something else that is being learned through the language. Faced with a class, any teacher will before long come to the conclusion that some pupils are better motivated than others. We recognize that people have different motives for learning. One person may be studying a language 'because he wants to,' another 'because he has to.' The former would probably be better motivated. Motivation has to do with the reasons for learning and with attitudes. In much teaching we set out to motivate the pupils through learning process itself. Teaching is planned so that learning becomes an interesting process.

It is not the teacher's effort to motivate the pupils but the pupils' own motivation that interests us. The reasons for learning a language may be diverse — to pass an examination, to use in one's job, to use on holiday in the country, as a change from watching television, because the educational system requires it, because one wants to know more of the culture and values of the foreign language group, because one wishes to make contact with the speakers of the language, because one hopes to live in the country concerned, and so on. Out of this diversity, a distinction has been made between two types of motivation — 'instrumental' and 'integrative.' The instrumentally motivated learner requires the language as a means to some other end. For the integrative learner the language and all that it brings by way of culture is an end in itself.

Attitudes are likely to be closely related to the reasons for learning. Integrative learners are likely to have very sympathetic attitudes towards the foreign culture and its speakers. With integrated motivation the learner sees himself as a potential member of the second language group.

Age

Aptitude is a stable and permanent characteristic of a learner. Motivation for language learning is not necessarily unchanging. With age comes a change in the potential for learning foreign languages. From the younger child, under the right conditions a higher level of proficiency can be expected.

Psychologists and linguists have attempted to formulate general theories of language learning and language use. To some learning is entirely the product of experience and our environment affects the same way. To others everybody has an innate language learning mechanism. It is only the environment we can manipulate in teaching.

The Social Function of Language

Language is a social activity. Choice of language varies according to social function and personal intention. Language teaching must provide the learner with means to select language which is suitable for the circumstances in which it is used and which is appropriate to express his personal states and ideas. The aims, methods and materials of language teaching vary according to the socio-linguistic status of the target language.

Few of us are aware of the range and variety of our uses of language even one typical day. Language will occur almost wherever we come into contact with other people and will be different according to the nature of the contact. Language also assails us even in situations in which no other people are present or when other people are present, but are not producing language for our consumption. Even people whose jobs may not appear to demand extensive use of language are placed in numerous situations which will require characteristic pieces of language. The linguist can study the relations between language forms and social context to understand how the individual's choice of language enables him to perform his social functions. Let us look at some important social functions on language use.

Dialect

The first set of influences produced dialect features. These are the product of the individual's geographical and class origin. Educational experience is also significant. If two speakers differ in grammar, pronunciation and vocabulary, we will conclude that they speak different dialects. Variation in pronunciation but not in grammar and vocabulary would be considered differences of accent. There is no clear quantitative linguistic measure to indicate where difference of dialect becomes difference of language. The issue is political and social. Everybody speaks a dialect. It is a social judgement that leads people to say that one English dialect is the 'correct' one. Dialect is not an important type of language variation for teaching.

Register

Our daily lives take us through a succession of activities requiring the use of language. The activities are very diverse. Whatever dialect we speak have specific features of language associated with them. Many activities are connected with our job.

Look at the life of any individual. We find that everyday he passes through a succession of roles. In each he will produce or hear features of language that are typical of the activity involved. For language teaching the roles with the most productive potential are the occupational roles. It is supposed that there are distinct varieties of language associated with people's occupations, and to these the name 'register' has been given. The language which one will use to talk about aeroplanes and flying will be quite unlike the language of people who work in and work with aeroplanes. The fact that one is talking about flying, a question of subject matter, will probably be indicated by vocabulary alone. A pilot's language will be marked by restrictions imposed on his range of grammar. It will also have a specialized vocabulary which will not have much resemblance to the vocabulary that one has been using.

One possible view of the aim of language teaching is that we are preparing the learner to perform a specific set of roles in a new language and new culture. Registers are potentially important in language teaching because many people do have an occupational purpose in learning a foreign language. The older a learner is the more likely it is that he knows why he is learning.

The Medium of Communication

Language contains fairly permanent features of dialect and more transitory features demanded by social roles. Just as we switch roles through the day. So we continually change the channel through which communication takes place. Choice of channel may sometimes be dependent on the previous choice of role. For most of us the auditory channel — speaking and hearing — used much more than the visual — reading and writing. In one day we use the visual medium to read the newspapers, books, letters, advertisements, notices in the bus and at work, our car instruction manual, or a football programme. Whether we do much writing depends on the nature of the job. The person who never has to write at work probably writes little more ever than the occasional letter. For many people, a good proportion of the working day is spent writing. As for speech, virtually all person-to-person contact involves uses of speech. Our family relationships, our leisure interests, and many occupational interactions are expressed in speech. Even when we are not producing language, we are often hearing it through radio, television, record player or film.

In language teaching generally one uniform style is taught, whether the aim is to teach, speech or writing. Instead of speech we teach 'spoken prose,' basing our uniform language on writing, not speech.

Status

The social relationships between participants in a language event are regularly marked by features of language. People are generally aware of their own 'status' in relation to one another. Our most intimate relationships are obviously with our own families. With friends and colleagues we are still informal but not to the same degree.

Status interacts with social dimensions. Written language is commonly formal. Status may be marked at any level of language.

In speech situation phonology may also be an indication of relative status. Deference thought due to a superior, or indifference to an inferior can be shown easily enough through intonation.

Language learning is not complete when we have acquired a 'general' language system. We can understand and make ourselves understood but we will not yet be producing entirely acceptable forms of language. There may be several semantically and grammatically acceptable ways of saying what we want to say but only one that is stylistically acceptable.

Situation

Language occurs predictably in situations like buying a railway ticket, ordering a meal, or making introductions. It will be less predictable in a law court.

Individual Intention and Social Function

Language teaching must be concerned with effective communication. Teachers should enable the pupil to acquire the means to achieve the maximum rhetorical effect for his spoken and written utterances. This will be difficult because there is no one-to-one relation between communication function and linguistic form.

People everywhere need to express the same kinds of motion. We need to display our emotions — surprise, pleasure, sorrow, anger, anxiety, hope, enthusiasm. We need to display our emotional reactions to others — sympathy, condolence, affection, admiration, trust, dislike, ridicule, insult. We need to display our attitudes and obligations — praise, blame, apologies, regret, promises, prohibitions, tolerance, permission, obligation. We have to express possibility, probability, necessity, likelihood, doubt, certainty, ability, agreement and disagreement, persuasion, suggestion, invitation, demands, orders, insistence, warnings, acceptance, caution, refusal, assertion, opposition, admission, emphasis, contrast, tact etc.

The Social Status of Non-native Languages

Getting educated is a personal matter, in contrast, providing education is a social enterprise. Society has its own reason for providing for the education of its young.

Second Language Learning

The language being learned (L2) can encompass part or all of government administration — politics, law, medicine, industry, internal trade, newspapers, general publishing and education. In education it may become the medium of instruction at any level from the primary school upwards. The greater the general use of the language in the country, the earlier in the educational system it is likely to become the medium of instruction.

In countries where the social role of English or French has been reduced as local languages have taken over, they have come to play an increasingly smaller part in the educational system too. India is a country in transition. English is losing its status as a second language, and in some states has already become a foreign language. It is now felt that the regional languages can cope with all aspects of education except technical and scientific subjects at the university level. Only in southern India does English remain a second language, because it can serve as a more acceptable lingua-franca than Hindi.

Foreign Language Learning

A foreign language learning situation is one in which the target language is not the mother-tongue of any group within the country and has no internal communication. The aim of teaching the language is to increase ease of contact with foreign language speakers outside the country. The provision of an adequate number of foreign language speakers is now thought necessary for a country's economy. The foreign language learner can form contacts with a community other than his own.

Foreign languages are taught in the secondary level school. Foreign language learning in many countries does not get beyond the stages of progressive accumulation of linguistic knowledge. The language teacher is the only person to provide exposure to the language. The learning process will be slow.

Alternate Language Learning

The society in which second and foreign language learners live will not normally provide them with any contact with native speakers of that language. The second language learner will use the language in his own country. The foreign language learner will not use the language at all in his own country, and only if he goes abroad will he have contact with native speakers. An 'alternate' language is like a second language in that it has a social function within the country of the learner. It is unlike a foreign language.

There are many well-publicized alternate language situations. English and French in Canada, English and Welsh in Wales, Hindi in non-Hindi speaking areas in India. Each of the language mentioned is the native language of one group and a target language for other groups in the country concerned. The related status of the languages in these situations is not necessarily one of equality. There are questions of geography and dominance.

The provision made for 'teaching' the alternate language may not be the most important factor in determining the "learning" of the language. Learning is a response to the enormous social pressures on the individual to use the language. Provided the social pressure is there, people will learn the language. People may learn an alternate language inspite of hostility towards it. Through one's language one is identified and identifies oneself with a particular social group. The acquisition of an alternate language offers an alternative to one's native group.

Discourse

A discourse is any connected speech or writing. A discourse may be produced by a single speaker or writer, or by two or more people engaging in a conversation, or in a written exchange. The study of discourse has become prominent in recent years, and the approaches are many and varied. Two fundamental terms in the study of discourse are cohesion and coherence. Cohesion is the presence of explicit linguistic links which provide recognizable structure such as she, this, after, therefore, and but; coherence is the degree to which a discourse makes sense in terms of our knowledge of the world.

Discourse Analysis

Discourse analysis is an approach to the study of discourse which is based upon traditional grammatical concepts and terms. In principle, we might apply the label discourse analysis or DA., to any kind of investigation of the structure of discourse. In practice the label is most commonly reserved for an approach based upon familiar grammatical concepts. In short D.A. is an attempt to extend our highly successful analysis of sentence structure to units rather than the sentence.

Displacement

Displacement is the ability to speak about things other than the here and the now. With just a single known exception every signal used by a non-human creature to communicate pertains wholly and directly to the immediate time and place of signalling. No non-human signal, with the marginal exception of scent markings left to define territory or to provide a trail, ever refers to the past or the future, to hypothetical or counterfactual states of affairs, or to anything not directly perceptible to the creature signalling. To put this more picturesquely, mice do not swap stories about their close encounters with cats, nor do bears soberly discuss the severity of the coming winter; rabbits do not engage in heated discussions about what might lie on the far side of the hill, nor do geese draw up plans for their next migration.

Human language is utterly different. We have not the slightest difficulty in taking about last night's football game or our own childhood. With ease we can discuss political events and so on. This is displacement; the ability to talk about things other than what we can see, hear, feel and smell at the moment. This displacement is one of the most momentous differences between human languages and the signalling system of all other species. They cannot do it at all; we do it almost every time we open our mouths. There is just one striking exception. A honeybee scout which has discovered a source of nectar returns to its hive and performs a dance, watched by the other bees. This bee dance tells the watching bees what direction the nectar lies in, how far away it is, and how much nectar there is. And this is displacement. The dancing bee is passing on information about a site which is visited sometime ago and watching it now cannot see, and the watching bees respond by flying off to locate the nectar. The bee dance is absolutely unique in the non-human world. No other creature can communicate anything of the sort. Even the bee dance is severely limited in its expressive powers. It cannot cope with the slightest novelty. The importance of displacement was first pointed out by the American linguist Charles Hockett in 1960.

Diglossia

Diglossia refers to marked specialization of function between two language varieties in a single speech community. It is by no means rare for two or more distinct languages or language varieties to be used side by side within a single community. For example many citizens of Spain routinely switch between Basque, Catalan or Galician on the one hand and Castilian Spanish on the other. German speakers in Germany, Switzerland and Austria switch between standard German and their own local varieties of German. All of English, Malay, Cantonese, Chinese and Tamil are widely spoken in Singapore, though very few people there can speak all four. People naturally prefer to speak their own mother tongue whenever they can. They switch to another language or variety only when they have to. In a few communities something different happens. The language or language varieties come to be perceived as having different functions in the community as a whole, and hence each variety is used more or less exclusively. Normally only two language varieties are involved in such a case and the result is diglossia. Diglossia was first identified as a distinctive phenomenon by the American linguist Charles Ferguson in the 1960s. Among the diglossic societies identified decades ago were Greece, German, Switzerland, the Arab countries and Paraguay. Changing political circumstances have brought diglossia to an end in Greece.

2

English as an International Language

For good or ill, at the end of the fifth full millennium since recorded history began, English is unique. Hundreds of millions of people use English everyday everywhere in the world. No language has ever before been put to so many uses so massively by so many people in so many places — on every continent and in every sea; in the air and in space; in thought, speech and writing; in print on paper and screen; in sound on tape and film; by radio, television, and telephone; and via electronic network and multi-media. It is also used as mother tongue or other tongue — fluently, adequately, or haltingly, constantly, intermittently, or seldom happily, unhappily or ambivalently — by over a billion people. Perhaps a fifth of the human race.

It has become difficult to travel anywhere in the world without finding English in daily use, especially in large cities. It dominates international popular culture. It is prominent in the everyday public life of many countries where it has acquired a secondary and often supernational function. English is the lingua-franca of airports and major hotels, of civil aviation and the shipping lanes. It is the leading language of science, medicine, technology and academic publication. Its US variety utterly dominates computer hardware, software, networking, e-mail and the vast creative chaos of cyberspace. Barriers of race, colour and creed are no hindrance to the continuing spread of the use of English.

Barbara M.H. Strang, Professor of English Language and General Linguistics at the University of Newcastle upon Tyne in England, described a tripartite model of English : ENL, ESL and

EFL. An influential variant of this classification was published by Randolph Quirk and Sidney Greenbaum of University College, London, Geoffrey Leech of the University of Lancaster, England, and Jan Svartik of the University of Lund, Sweden, the editors of the leading reference grammar of the 1970s. Without using Strang's letter categories, they put the matter as follows : "English is the world's most widely used language. It is useful to distinguish three primary categories of use : as a native language. as a second language and as a foreign language."

English as L_1 and L_2

It is arguable that native speakers of English can no longer make strong proprietary claims to the language which they now share with most of the developed world. The English language was taken on a number of regional forms. A number of world varieties of English exist : British, American, Carribbean, West African, East African, Indian, South-East Asian, Australasian and so on. Within these broad varieties there are dialects. Of these geographically disparate varieties of English there are two kinds : those of first language situations where English is the Mother Tongue (MT) as in the USA or Australasia, and Second Language (SL) situations where English is the language of commercial, administrative and educational institutions. Each variety of English marks a speech community.

These are two main kinds of motivation in foreign language learning : instrumental and integrative. When anyone learns a foreign language instrumentally, he needs it for operational purposes — to be able to read books in the new language, to be able to communicate with other speakers of the language. The tourist, the salesman, the science student are clearly motivated to learn English instrumentally. When anyone learns a foreign language for integrative purposes, he is trying to identify much more closely with a speech community. In a second language learning situation, English is the language of the mass media, the language of official institutions, of law courts, local and central government, of education. It is also the language of large commercial and industrial organizations. Clearly a good command of English in a second language situation is the passport to social and economic advancement. The successful user of the appropriate variety of English identifies himself as a successful integrated member of that language community.

English as a Foreign Language

The role of English within a nation's daily life is influenced by geographical, historical, cultural and political factors. The role of English at a given point in time must affect both the way it is taught and the resultant impact on the daily life and growth of the individual. The place of English in the life of many second and foreign language learners today is much less easy to define than it was some years ago. Michael West viewed in 1963 : 'The foreigner is learning English to express ideas rather than emotion; for his emotional expression he has the mother-tongue.... It is a useful general rule that intensive words and items are of secondary importance to a foreign learner however common they may be.' This remains true for learners in extreme foreign language situations. Learners of English as a foreign language have a choice of language variety to a larger extent than second language learners. The Japanese situation is one in which both British and American varieties are equally acceptable and both are taught. The choice of variety is partly influenced by the availability of teachers, partly by geographical location and political influence. Foreign students of English in Mexico and the Philippines tend to learn American English. Europeans tend to learn British-English. The decreasing role of English in India and Sri Lanka has made for a shift of emphasis to change a long established second language situation to something nearer to a foreign language situation.

English in India

English plays a key role in our educational system and national life. The British introduced English in our educational system in order to produce cheap clerks for their colonial administration and to produce, what Lord Macaulay called "a class of people, Indian in blood and colour, but English in taste, in opinions, in morals and in intellect." English helped the growth of nationalism which ultimately freed India from foreign fetters. Indian national leaders drew inspiration from the writings of the great thinkers who wrote in English. English is rich in literature and culture. English served as a great unifying force in India's freedom struggle. English is a link language. It has greatly contributed to the advancement of learning. It reflects in our ways and views. The teaching of English should be made more practical and language-oriented. We need knowledge of English for different purposes. English is to be taught as language of comprehension rather than as literary language. The objectives of teaching English at the school stage may be summed up :

(1) to understand English with ease when spoken at normal conversational speed;
(2) to speak English fluently and correctly;
(3) to read English with comprehension and at a reasonable speed so as to use it as a library, language for gathering information and for the pleasures of reading;
(4) to write neatly and correctly;
(5) to appreciate poetry;
(6) to acquire knowledge of the elements of English for practical command of the language;
(7) to translate common English words, phrases and sentences into their functional equivalents in mother tongue and vice versa;
(8) to develop interest in English;
(9) to expose the learners to real life situations.

The major areas of the school curriculum are the instruments by which the individual grows into a more secure, more contributory and more total member of the society. It is hardly surprising that more teaching hours are devoted to English in the class rooms of the world than to any other subject in the curriculum. One should not wink at the teaching of English.

Bilingualism

In modern western society the ability to speak two languages is often seen as something of a remarkable achievement, particularly in the English speaking countries. Over seventy per cent of the world's population are thought to be bilingual or multilingual. There is good reason to believe that bilingualism or multilingualism has been the norm for most human beings at least for the last few millennia. There is evidence that children raised bilingually tend to be more expressive, more original and better communicators than children raised with only one language. Bilingualism can be the property of an individual, but equally it can be the property of an entire speech community in which two or more languages are routinely used. The existence of bilingual and multilingual societies raises serious social, political and educational issues. Difference of opinion lead to language conflict.

SLA Theories

Second Language Learners of different ages have different characteristics and access to different conditions for learning. A general theory of SLA will need to account for language acquisition by learners with a variety of characteristics, learning in a variety of different contexts.

According to the behaviourists all learning takes place through the same underlying process, habit formation. Learners receive linguistic input from speakers in their environment and positive reinforcement for their correct repetitions and imitations. As a result habits are formed. Because language development is described as the acquisition of a set of habits, a person learning a second language starts off with the habits associated with his first language. These habits interfere with those needed for second language speech, and new habits must be formed.

For the behaviourists, errors are seen as first language habits interfering with the acquisition of second language habits. This psychological learning theory has often been linked to the Contrastive Analysis Hypothesis (CAH). The CAH predicts that where there are similarities between the two languages, the learner will acquire target language structures with ease. Researchers have found that not all errors predicted by the CAH are actually made. Learners do make many errors which are not predictable on the basis of the CAH.

The behaviourist account has proven to be at best an incomplete explanation of SLA. Psychologists and language acquisition researchers have moved as to new, more complex theories of learning.

Cognitive psychologists tend to see SLA as the building up of knowledge systems that can eventually be called on automatically for speaking and understanding. At first, learners have to pay attention to any aspect of the language which they are trying to understand or produce. Gradually, through experience and practice, learners become able to use certain parts of their knowledge quickly and automatically.

Cognitive psychologists have also investigated a phenomenon they call 'restructuring'. This refers to the observation that sometimes things which we know and use automatically may not be explained in terms of a gradual build-up of automaticity through practice. They seem rather to be based on the interaction of knowledge we already have or on the acquisition of new knowledge which somehow 'fits' into an existing system and may 'restructure' this system. This may lead to sudden bursts of progress for the learner.

Cognitive theory is a relative newcomer to SLA research. The theory itself cannot easily predict what kinds of structures will be automatized through practices and what will be restructures. The direct applications of cognitive theory for classroom teaching are premature. Cognitive theory is not able to predict which first language structures will be transferred and which will not.

Some linguists have proposed a position similar to Chomsky's ideas on first language learning. This is called the creative construction hypothesis. Learners are thought to 'construct' internal representations as 'mental pictures' of the target language. The internal representations are thought to develop in the direction of the full second language system. Most of the evidence of this theory has come from the analysis of learners' errors at various points in their second language acquisition and the order or sequence in which certain structures are acquired.

Creative construction hypothesis proposes that internal processing strategies operate on language input without any direct dependence on the learner actually producing the language. The learner need not actually speak or write in order to acquire language. Acquisition takes place internally as learners read and hear samples of the language that they understand. The speech and writing which the learner eventually produces is seen as an outcome of the learning process rather than as the cause of learning or as a necessary step in learning. Learners' oral or written production is useful only in so far as it allows the learner to participate in communicative situations. The creative construction theory which has had the most influence on second language teaching is the one proposed by Stephen Krashen (1982).

Krashen has developed an overall theory of second language acquisition which attempts to bring together research findings from a number of diverse areas. Five central hypotheses constitute his 'monitor model.' They are (i) the acquisition-learning hypothesis, (ii) the monitor hypothesis, (iii) the natural order hypothesis, (iv) the input hypothesis, (v) the affective filter hypothesis.

According to Krashen there are two ways for adult second language learners to approach a second language. They may 'acquire' it or they may 'learn' it. We acquire as we engage in meaningful interaction in the second language with no attention to form. We learn via a conscious process of study and attention to form and error correction. For Krashen acquisition is by far the more important process. He asserts that it is only acquired knowledge which is readily available for natural, fluent communication. It is extremely difficult to detect which system, acquisition or learning, is at work at any given moment.

Krashen argues that the acquired system acts to initiate the speaker's utterances and is responsible for fluency and intuitive judgements about correctness. The learned system acts only as an editor or 'monitor.' Krashen has specified three conditions necessary for monitor use : sufficient time, focus on form, and knowing the rules. It is very difficult to show evidence of 'monitor' use. In any given utterance, it is impossible to determine what has been produced by the acquired system and what is the result of monitor use.

The natural order hypothesis states that we acquire the rules of a language in a predictable sequence. Some rules are acquired early while others are acquired late. Contrary to intuition, the rules which are easier to state are not necessarily the first to be acquired. Most of the evidence for this hypothesis comes from the morpheme studies.

Krashen asserts that we acquire language in only one way — by receiving comprehensive input, that is by understanding messages.

If the input contains forms and structures just beyond the learner's current level of competence in the language, then both comprehension and acquisition will occur. Krashen admits that comprehensible input is a necessary but not a sufficient condition for acquisition.

The 'affective filter' is an imaginary barrier which prevents learners from using input which is available in the environment. 'Affect' refers to such things as motives, needs, attitudes and emotional states. A learner who is tense, angry, anxious or bored will screen out input, making it unavailable for acquisition. Thus depending on the learner's state of mind, the filter limits what is attended to and what is acquired. The filter will be 'up' or operating when the learner is stressed, self-conscious or unmotivated. It will be 'down' when the learner is relaxed and motivated. The affective filter hypothesis appears to have immediate implications for classroom practice. Teachers can understand why some learners, given the same opportunity to learn, may be successful while others are not.

Proponents of the interactionist view (such as Michael Long) agree with Krashen that comprehensible input is necessary for language acquisition. However, they are more concerned with the question of 'how' input is made comprehensible. They see interactional modifications which take place in conversations between native speakers and non-native speakers as the necessary mechanism for this to take place. For Long and others, modified interaction must be necessary for language use. Interactional modification makes input comprehensible. Comprehensible input promotes acquisition. Therefore interactional modification promotes acquisition.

Behaviourism

Behaviourism is the theory that psychology should invoke only observable and measurable phenomena. Early in the twentieth century, psychology had become somewhat obscurantist (reactionary) and even metaphysical. Behaviourism originated as a healthy reaction to this state of affairs. The early behaviourists wanted to sweep away what they saw as empty speculation and the endless postulation of undetectable concepts.

Behaviourism exercised great influence over the linguist Leonald Bloomfield and the American structuralists who followed him. In 1957 the American psychologist B.F. Skinner published *Verbal Behaviour.* It was an attempt at interpreting language acquisition strictly in terms of behaviourism. It was the most radical attempt ever at treating language in a behaviourist framework. Skinner's book was savagely reviewed by Noam Chomsky. He argued that Skinner's approach not only explained nothing but could not possibly explain anything of interest. Chomsky's review persuaded a whole generation of linguists that the essentially theoretical behaviourist approach and nothing to offer linguistics. As a result, the linguists influenced by Chomsky abandoned behaviourism and embraced mentalism. Linguistics was eventually integrated into the emerging discipline of cognitive science.

D.A. Wilkins views that for behaviourists, there is not a theory of language learning as such but merely the application to language of general principles of learning. In general terms, there is no difference between the way one learns a language and the way one learns to do anything else. It follows that learning is controlled by the condition under which it takes place, and as long as individuals are subjected to the same conditions, they will learn in the same way. What appears to be language learning ability is really no more than different learning experience.

Every utterance and every part of an utterance is produced as the result of the presence of some kind of 'stimulus'. The stimulus may be physically present in the situation. It may be verbal. It may be internal. As long as a child is making correct responses he can be reinforced and will learn. If he made only correct responses he would learn that much more rapidly. In practice he may utter incorrect forms. Having learned that *filled* is the past tense of *fill,* he may overgeneralize this response and apply it to *sell.* In learning a language one has to acquire both 'informal' and a 'thematic' repertoire of responses.

Most developments in language teaching since the Second World War have been based on the assumption that language is a form of behaviour. Even when where there is no explicit statement of a theoretical foundations of a method, the underlying attitude can be inferred from the use of such terms as 'skill' or 'habit.' Foreign language learning is basically a mechanical process of habit formation. Learning the language is like learning to type, to ride a bicycle, or to carry out any other routines that we characterize as habits.

A behaviourist method of language teaching should embody at least the following principles. It should be firmly anchored in spoken language. We might expect an even greater salience to be given to speech. The teaching of writing would follow the teaching of spoken language. We should expect a great deal of language activity by the pupils themselves.

The teacher would appear to be giving a considerable amount of assistance to the learner to get his responses right. At first the class may be doing no more than imitate what the teacher was saying. The practice would proceed rapidly. Drills are a form of practice, exercises are a form of test.

Reinforcement should follow the response as quickly as possible. In the classroom it might appear in the form of approval from the teacher or satisfaction by the pupil that he has got his response right. The notion of immediate reinforcement is employed most powerfully in language laboratory drilling. The tape is produced to provide a sequence of stimulus-response-reinforcement. It further meets the requirements of the behaviourist model by demanding from each pupil numerous repetitions of correct spoken responses. In the classroom the teacher is present to judge the appropriateness of a response and a certain amount of flexibility is permissible. In the laboratory, the learner is alone with the material. He has to evaluate his own performance and provide his own reinforcement. Whether in classroom or laboratory, behaviourist teaching relies more on analogy than on rules for teaching the structure of the language.

Mentalism/Cognitivism

Mentalism is the doctrine that the mind can be invoked in scientific investigation and even be made the object of study itself. Today most psychologists, philosophers and linguists, are preferably happy to invoke invisible things like minds and purposes and even to make mind itself the object of study. This approach is called mentalism.

Everybody learns a language because they possess an inborn capacity which permits them to acquire a language. This capacity is by definition universal. In a sense, mentalists too argue that language learning is the same for everybody. For the mentalists, what the learners share is a capacity, the existence of which the behaviourists would deny. For the mentalists, language is far too complex a form of behaviour to be accounted for in terms of features external to the individual. Chomsky attacks the notion that language responses are under the control of external stimuli, that the individual is merely the locus of behaviour. Since all normal human beings learn their language successfully, they must possess some internal capacity for language that other animals do not have. Since this capacity cannot have been acquired socially, it must be innate. It is the willingness to admit the possible existence of unobservable internal mechanism that leads these linguists to be considered mentalistic. They would argue that the nature of language is such that it is impossible to explain it without postulating an innate mechanism of a fairly well-defined kind. To the innate mechanism they propose the name 'Language Acquisition Device' (LAD).

Whereas the behaviourists will talk of the child using 'analogy' in the construction of sentences, the mentalists prefer to think in terms of the production and application of 'rules.'

It is a matter of fact that behaviourism has influenced foreign language teaching. Whether or not mentalist attitudes will be equally influential is a matter for conjecture. A language teaching methodology is not something to be derived directly from a linguistic theory.

There is the notion that the learning process is essentially uninfluenced by external factors. Carefully planned schedules of reinforcement are unnecessary since learning will take place whether or not the individual is reinforced. There is no need for the amount of active participation in language production that the behaviourists and others require. Learning can take place without repetitions and active responding. Learning involves the internal mastery of the rule. The learning mechanism operates through its capacity to formulate rules about the language once the individual has been exposed to it. The essential condition is exposure to the language.

As long as the exposure continues the learning mechanism will operate. The greater the exposure to language, the more effectively the learner can formulate and revise his hypotheses about the structure of the language.

The material of language teaching should be extensive samples of natural language. The linguistic range that the child would meet would be enormous. The learning of a foreign language should be a meaningful activity throughout.

Language teachers need not feel obliged to adopt either behaviourism or mentalism. Foreign language learning can be considered a matter of both nature and nurture. Language teachers cannot ignore factors that might speed the learning process. The only thing we can influence are the externals. What goes on inside the individuals is beyond us. Our experience suggests that the environment that we create for learning has a considerable effect on how well the children are able to use the language. Using language requires choices all the time. A belief in 'learning through doing' demands that practice in exercising those choices should be an important part of language teaching. The answer to the questions, Mentalism or Behaviourism is Mentalism and Behaviourism.

3

Linguistics

Linguistics is the scientific study of language. There were significant traditions of language study in ancient India, in ancient Greece and Rome, among the medieval Arabs and Jews and elsewhere. Most of these investigations were solely confined to studying the local prestige language. Modern linguistics does not derive from these older traditions. Instead, it grew up from fresh beginnings in Europe and the U.S.A. By the seventeenth century a few European scholars and philosophers were beginning to interest themselves in general questions about the nature of language. Between the seventeenth and nineteenth century scholars like Descrates, Locke and Homboldt made a number of significant contributions. With a few exceptions, these men typically knew nothing about any languages other than the major language of Europe. Their work suffered from a lack of data. Much of it was speculative and a priori. By the end of the eighteenth century historical linguistics had begun to be firmly established. Throughout the nineteenth century the historical study of language was for many people synonymous with the scientific study of language. Towards the end of the century a number of linguists began turning their attention to the serious study of the structure of language from a non-historical perspective. The most influential figure was the Swiss linguist Ferdinand de Saussure.

Saussure had been trained as a historical linguist. He had made major contributions to historical studies. He began to focus on some more general questions of language structure. After his death his former students edited their lecture notes into a book which was published under Saussure's name in 1916. This book is the famous *Cours.* Saussure has been dubbed "the father of linguistics." The

European linguistic tradition, with its heavy theoretical bias, largely, derives from Saussure's work. In Britain Bronislaw Malinowski and J.R. Firth independently developed a more strongly data-oriented descriptive approach born out of anthropological fieldwork.

In the USA anthropologists were undertaking the study of the dying native American languages. This study was keenly promoted by Fraus Boas who is regarded as the founder of the American linguistic tradition. Boas' successors such as A.L. Kroeber and Edward Sapir went on to develop linguistics as an independent discipline in the USA. But the single most influential figure was Leonald Bloomfield. In 1957 a young American linguist Noam Chomsky published *Syntactic Structures.* Chomsky made a number of revolutionary proposals. He introduced the idea of generative grammar. He developed a particular kind of generative grammar called 'transformational grammar.' He laid the foundations for integrating the field into as yet unnamed new discipline of cognitive science. His ideas excited a whole generation of students. Today Chomsky's influence is undimmed.

Linguistics today is surely as lively a discipline as any on earth. In the last fifty years or so we have probably learned more about language than our ancestors managed in two thousand years. And there is no reason to believe that things are slowing down now.

What is Linguistics?

According to Robins 'linguistics is concerned with human language as a universal and recognizable part of the human behaviour and of the human faculties perhaps one of the most essential to human life as we know it and one of the far-reaching of human capabilities in relation to the whole span of mankind's achievements.' It sounds a little abstract. There is no way of studying language without referring to and taking examples from particular languages. Linguistics does not emphasise practical knowledge or mastery of a particular language. Linguists may know only one language, or may know several, or may even study a language they do not know at all. What they are trying to study are the ways in which language is organized to fulfil human needs, as a system of communication. There is a difference between a person who knows many languages (called a polyglot) and a linguist who studies general principles of language organization and language behaviour.

In short linguistics is learning about language rather than learning a language. This distinction is often explained as the difference between learning how a car works and learning how to drive a car. We learn a set of habits and do some practice. This is similar to learning how to speak a language. When we learn how the car works, we open up its mechanism, study it and investigate the relationship of its parts to one another. This is similar to what we do in scientific study of language or linguistics. We investigate the mechanism of language, its parts and how all these parts fit together to perform particular functions.

Every language is a system. It does not matter which language we take up to illustrate the working of language in human life. In the past the study of language was considered to be the study of the grammar of some prestigious classical language. Today we consider all language as fit objects of language study.

Linguistics as a Science

Linguistics can be understood as a science in both general and specific terms. Generally we use the term "science" for any knowledge that is based on clear systematic and rational understanding. We also use the term for the systematic study of phenomena enabling us to state some principles or theories regarding the phenomenon. This study proceeds by examination of publicly verifiable data obtained through observation of phenomena and experimentation. In other words it is empirical and objective. Science must also provide explanation after adequate observation of data which should be consistent and economical. There should be no contradictions between definite parts of the explanation or statement. These criteria of science can be applied to linguistics.

Linguistics studies language. Language is a phenomenon which is both objective and variable. It has a concrete shape and occurrence. The linguist studies the components of language. Observation leads to processes of classification and definition. Linguistics observes the features of language, classifies these features as being sound features of particular types, or words belonging to particular classes on the basis of similarity or differences with other sounds and words.

Linguistics is also social science because it studies language which is a form of social behaviour and exists in interaction between human beings in society. Language is also linked to human mental processes. Linguistics is a human discipline since it is concerned with human language. It is a part of the study of the humanities as well. Linguistics is central to all areas of knowledge.

Scope of Linguistics

Linguistics today is a subject of study independent of other disciplines. Before the twentieth century, the study of language was not regarded as a separate area of study in its own right. It was considered to be a part of studying the history of language or the philosophy of language. This was known not as linguistics, but as philosophy. So 'linguistics' is a modern name which defines a specific discipline. In it we study language not in relation to some other area such as history or philosophy but language as itself, as a self-enclosed and autonomous system, worthy of study in its own right. The main concern of modern linguistics is to describe language, to study its nature and to establish a theory of language. Linguistics aims at studying the components of the language system and to ultimately arrive at an explanatory statement as how the system works.

Descriptive Linguistics

Descriptive linguistics is emphasised in modern linguistics as it is the fundamental aspect of the study of language. It contrasts with prescriptive linguistics of earlier times. It deals with description of how language actually works, rather than how it should be. In descriptive linguistics we describe the language at all levels, *i.e.*, phonology, grammar, and semantics. We analyse and describe the structure of the language. Modern descriptive linguistics is based on a structural approach to language.

Robins defines : 'Descriptive linguistics is concerned with the description and analysis of the ways in which a language operates and is used by a given set of speakers at a given time.'

Modern linguistics is mainly descriptive.

Comparative Linguistics

Comparative linguistics is concerned with comparing two or more languages. When the history of these languages is compared with a view to discovering the historical relation between these languages, it is known as comparative historical study. This kind of study was dominant in the nineteenth century.

As modern languages are held to have descended from ancient languages, historical comparative linguistics describes this process of evolution and development as well as similarities in the process of this language change. A language from which other languages have developed is called a proto language or a parent language. Languages that develop from it are in a sense later stages of this protolanguage and these languages are sister languages. All these taken together form a language family. This protolanguage is not something that exists now. It is reconstructed by historical linguists on the basis of written records, coins, inscriptions etc. It can never be reconstructed completely.

Historical Linguistics

Historical linguistics is the study of language change and of its consequences. Historical linguistics was the first branch of linguistics to be placed on a firm scholarly footing. It is traditional to date the founding of the discipline to 1786 when the British amateur linguist Sir William Jones famously pointed out the clear common ancestry of Greek, Latin and Sanskrit, and hence of the existence of the vast Indo-European family of languages, all of which descend from a single common ancestor.

Historical linguistics was vigorously developed throughout the nineteenth century. In recent years there has been an explosion of interest in all aspects of language change. Linguists have been searching eagerly for principles governing language change.

Psycholinguistics

Psycholinguistics is the study of the connection between language and mind. Language is a mental phenomenon. It is mental processes that are articulated in language behaviour. Psycholinguistics studies these mental processes — processes of thought and concept formation and their articulation in language.

Psycholinguistics began to emerge as a distinct discipline in the 1950s. To some extent its emergence was promoted by the insistence of Noam Chomsky that linguistics should be regarded as a part of congnitive psychology. There were other factors as well, notably the growing interest in the question of language acquisition by children. Cognitive psychology is the area which explores how meanings are understood by the human brain, how syntax and memory are linked, how messages are decoded and stored.

Psycholinguistics also studies the influence of psychological factors such as intelligence, motivation, anxiety etc. on the kind of language that is understood and produced. For instance, in the case of errors made by a speaker, there may be psychological reasons which influence comprehension or production that are responsible for the occurrence of an error. Our perception of speech sounds or graphic symbols is influenced by the state of our mind. Psycholinguistics can offer some insights and corrective measures for this condition.

Psycholinguistics is concerned with the learning of language at various stages : the early acquisition of a first language by children and later stages in acquisition of first and other languages. Psycholinguists attempt to answer questions such as whether the human brain has an inborn language ability structured in such a way that certain grammatical and semantic patterns are embedded in it. Psycholinguistic studies in language acquisition are very useful in the area of language teaching. They help teachers to understand error production and individual differences among learners and thus devise appropriate syllabi and materials for them.

One specialized area within psycholinguistics is neurolinguistics that studies the psychological basis of language and language disorders.

Sociolinguistics

Sociolinguistics is the branch of linguistics which studies the relation between language and society. The social aspect of language attracted early attention notably from the great Swiss linguist Ferdinand de Saussure at the beginning of the twentieth century. But it was perhaps only in the 1950s that serious investigation began. The key figure is the American linguist William Labov. In the 1960s he began a series of investigations of variation in language.

Sociolinguistics may be defined as the study of variation in language, or more precisely variation within speech communities. In a speech community of any size, there is considerable variation among individuals : stockbrokers do not speak like plumbers, women do not speak like men, young people do not speak like old people and so on. Moreover, even a single individual is not confined to a single variety of the language : you do not use the language in the same way when you are chatting to friends, when you are interviewed for a job, when you are writing an essay etc. Earlier linguists dismissed this variation as peripheral, as inconsequential, even as nuisance getting in the way of good descriptions. Today we recognize that variation is an integral part of language.

Sociolinguistics is based on the fact that language is not a single homogeneous entity, but has different forms in different situations. The changes in language occur because of changes in social conditions, social class, gender, regional and cultural groups etc. A particular social group may speak a different variety of a language from the rest of the community. This group becomes a speech community.

Variation in language may occur because the speakers belong to a different geographical region. Taking the example of English, we find that it is not a single language but exists in the form of several varieties. One kind of English is called RP. This kind of English is used in the South West of England and particularly associated with the Universities of Oxford and Cambridge, and the BBC. It is an educated and formal kind of English. But there are other varieties of the English that is spoken in the North of England, in Yorkshire and Lancashire, in Scotland (Scottish English); Wales (Welsh English) etc. A less educated variety of English is that spoken by working class people in London often called Cockney English. Then there are the varieties of English spoken by people of different countries around the world *e.g.*, American English, Indian English, Australian English.

Anthropological Linguistics

Anthropological linguistics is the study of the relation between language and culture. Anthropologists generally find it necessary to learn the language of the people they are studying. They realized early that the languages themselves might provide valuable clues about the cultures under investigation. In the early nineteenth century the anthropologist Franz Boas in the USA laid particular stress upon the importance of native American languages in the study of native American cultures. Thanks to his influence and that of his student Edward Sapir American linguistics was largely born out of anthropology. In Britain the anthropologist Bronislaw Malinowski drew comparable attention to the study of language in the early twentieth century. His idea greatly influenced J.R. Firth, widely regarded as the founder of linguistics in Britain.

Anthropological linguistics is now recognized as a distinctive discipline. It is also called linguistic anthropology.

The structure of language has a social and cultural basis. Each culture organizes its world in its own way. Language becomes a way of embodying the world views and beliefs of a culture and the things that culture holds sacred. Anthropological studies have explored the relation between language and culture. Language is invented to communicate and express a culture. The language begins to determine the way we think and see the world. The language is the means by which we understand and think about the world. These aspects of language and culture are still being discussed by anthropological linguists, philosophers of language and ethnographers.

Applied Linguistics

Applied linguistics is the application of the concepts and methods of linguistics to any of various practical problems involving language. The term 'applied linguistics' is often encountered in connection with foreign language teaching. Linguistic concepts find a number of uses here — the systematic comparison of the sounds, the words and the grammatical systems of the mother tongue and the language being learned.

Linguistics has also proved useful in a variety of other practical domains such as mother-tongue teaching, lexicography, translation, the teaching of reading, and the diagnosis and treatment of language disability. Today all these are understood as forming part of applied linguistics.

Linguistics in Language Teaching

Linguistics has different aims from language teaching. Linguists set out to study the human language faculty, to develop theories to explain language behaviour, to provide the most efficient means for describing languages and to make the most of accurate and comprehensive descriptions of languages available. It is quite wrong to argue that developments in linguistics should cause changes in language teaching. The relationship cannot be one of cause and effect. In making language teaching decisions it is wrong to refer only to evidence drawn from linguistics. Language teaching is a pragmatic business. We cannot ignore strongly held beliefs about what constitute the most effective approaches to language teaching. What seems good linguistics might turn out to be bad psychology. The teaching of reading could well be an instance of this. The teacher is the only person who has to take all the evidence into account. It is perfectly possible to argue that at times the application of linguistics to language teaching has been a misuse of linguistics. The very term 'applied linguistics' is open to an interpretation which suggest that language teaching is somehow derived from linguistics. D.A. Wilkins staunchly records that the teacher must retain his critical faculties in his use of linguistic notions. According to him the relationship of linguistics to language teaching must be studied afresh. Past practice cannot just be continued with a change in the points to be applied.

Insights

According to D.A. Wilkins 'insights' are linguistic notions that increase one's understanding of the nature of language and consequently of the nature of language learning. Language teaching decisions have to be taken at many different levels — defining the goals of learning, determining the broad methodological approach, assessing the value of particular techniques, organizing the language content. For the language teacher the study of linguistics is probably more rewarding in this respect than in any other. Linguistics defines the relationship between speech and writing. In defining his aims a teacher will find it informative to look at the langue-parole distinction. He also has to decide how far the language he teaches should replicate the speech of actual utterances. He should also see how far the language should be an idealized or standardized form of language. With the real understanding of such differences he is in a better position to judge whether the approach he has adopted is likely to produce the result he wants.

Sometimes the insights provided by the linguists are not really novel. There are times when important notions remain unexpressed or are taken for granted. The centrality of grammatical structure in language learning is a case in point. There was a period when language learning reacted strongly to the practical uselessness of much of the language taught in traditional courses. The solution was seen in the selection of a more useful vocabulary, and teaching materials were constructed to facilitate the systematic introduction of this vocabulary.

It is our knowledge of grammar that provides what Chomsky has called our 'rule-governed activity.' This is every speaker's ability to understand and construct grammatically correct sentences that he has not previously met in the language. Our language competence consists of the ability to recognize and construct grammatically correct sentences appropriate to the circumstances of utterance. If we do not know the rules of language well enough to be able to make new sentences, we have not yet learned that language. Any other kind of language performance, involving the uttering of remembered phrases and sentences, is not true language behaviour but only language-like behaviour. We need to evaluate our methods according to their success in producing real competence in language. It is a learner's creativity that we should investigate when we are testing his language ability.

Implications

Everyday in his classroom work the language teacher makes scores of decisions, some prepared, some off the cuff, about his methods and techniques. Many decisions have been taken for him by the curriculum designers. The decisions about teaching all aim to improve the process of 'learning.' Everyone of the decisions in teaching has in it a view on learning.

Let us suppose that a new word or collocation occurs. There is a multitude of options open to the teacher. To teach the meaning of the item he may translate it. This implies the belief that learning a foreign language is learning to map it on to the mother-tongue. Alternatively he may present the item together with one or more visual images. This implies that meaning is simply the product of recurring associations. He may exemplify in numerous sentences. This implies that learning is an inductive process. He may explain the item. This implies that learning is the application of cognitive skills. Having presented the item in one or other of these ways, he may do no more. This implies that language learning does not require productive participation by the learner. He may ask for repetitions. This implies that the active production of item is necessary to learning. He may ask for numerous repetitions. This implies that learning is strengthened in proportion to the number of times that an item is produced. He may ask the pupils to select an appropriate item from among a number of alternatives offered. This implies that learning language is learning to exercise choices.

There is a relation between language teaching and language acquisition. In any real situation, implications are not the only ones that operate. Translation is generally a 'bad' thing for the teaching of meaning. This does not mean that one never presents an item in association with its mother-tongue translation. There are occasions when it is more desirable to obtain a rapid and easy interpretation. One might not want to interrupt a highly motivating narrative. One might plump for the efficacy of a quick translation.

Language teaching aims to be practically effective, not theoretically consistent. The study of linguistics, especially theories of language acquisition, helps to articulate the implications of many current and proposed practices in language teaching.

Applications

The relation of application is the easiest to understand. There will be cases where notions and information drawn from linguistics act directly upon the process of language teaching. This is the relation that is implied in the term 'applied linguistics.' Most language teachers who study linguistics expect to derive applications from it. Language descriptions provide the input to the construction of teaching materials. What the teacher expects is that linguistics will offer him quite new and very different descriptions of the language that he teaches. He also expects that linguistic description will extend the range of his knowledge of the language.

The notion that teaching should reflect the form of description is one that recurs and from time to time is applied with varying degrees of rigidity. In the forms of language description being proposed in the 1940s and 1950s, there was to be no difference between the manner in which the linguist proceeded in analysing a language and the analysis that he finally produced. He was to start with the phonetics of the language, proceed to the phonology, then to the morphology and eventually to the syntax. The analysis would be carried out with as little reference to meaning as possible. The study of semantics would follow the analysis of forms.

We refer to linguistics in an attempt to make the process of change in language teaching less subject to fashion and more dependent on the cumulative increase in our knowledge of language learning and teaching. It is necessary to refer to linguistics for more than a description of the language we are teaching. Linguistic arguments have to be properly placed in relation to psychological and general educational arguments. The real contribution of linguistics is to increase one's understanding of the nature of language. Anyone who has studied linguistics is standardized to language and thereby to the complexity of language learning. Language teaching still depends very heavily on the infinitive interpretations that the teacher constantly has to make, interpretations of learning and of language. The study of linguistics roots those intuitions in a more complete understanding of language. The linguistically sophisticated teacher's judgement is better informed.

It would be absurd to pretend that no one can be a good language teacher unless he has a knowledge of linguistics. It is possible that linguistics is not even one of the most important elements in the preparation of a language teacher. The value of linguistics is that, by increasing the awareness of his language, it makes him more competent and therefore a better language teacher.

Levels of Linguistic Analysis

Language has a hierarchical structure. It is made up of units which are themselves made up of smaller units which are made of still smaller units till we have the smallest indivisible unit — a phoneme. In short phonemes combine together to make larger units of sounds; these combine into larger meaningful unit called a morpheme; morphemes combine to form larger units of words; words combine to form a larger unit or sentence; several sentences combine to make a unified piece of speech or writing which we call a text or discourse. At each stage or level, there are certain rules that operate which permit the occurrence and combination of smaller units. So we can say that rules of phonology determine the occurrence and combination of particular phonemes; rules of word formation cover the behaviour of particular morphemes, rules of word formation determine the combination and positioning of words in a sentence. Each level is a system in its own right.

The levels of language structure are not completely separate from one another. There are important vital linkages between the levels. We can study these links only after we describe and analyse structure at each level separately. Thus phonetics studies language at the level of sounds. Phonology studies the combination of sounds into organized units of speech, the formation of syllabus, and larger units. Morphology studies the patterns of formation of words by the combination of sounds into distinctive units of meaning called morphemes. Syntax is the level at which we study how words combine to form phrases, phrases combine to form clauses, and clauses join to make sentences. Semantics deals with the level of meaning in language. An extension of the study of semantics is pragmatics. Pragmatics deals with the contextual aspects of meaning in particular situations. Discourse is the study of chunks of language which are bigger than a simple sentence.

In addition to these levels of linguistic analysis, we also study graphology which is the study of the writing system of a language and the conventions used in representing speech in writing. Lexicology studies the manner in which lexical items (words) are grouped together as in the compilation of dictionaries.

Some linguists consider the proper area of linguistics to be confined to the levels of phonology, morphology and syntax. This is called microlinguistics. Some take a macro linguistic view which includes the other levels of language as well as other aspects of language.

Structuralist Linguistics

Structuralist linguistics arose in the 1930s as a result of two needs felt by the academic community in the U.S.A. First, there was a general feeling of dissatisfaction with 'traditional grammar.' Secondly linguists in the USA were faced by a severe practical problem : the description and preservation of the native Indian languages before they literally died out.

For the structuralist, language was a system of speech sounds, arbitrarily assigned to the objects, states and concepts to which they referred, used for human communication. From this four axioms can be derived : (1) Language is speech. This is in direct contrast with traditional linguistics which relegated speech to a position of secondary importance, after writing. The structuralist reversed the order declaring 'The Speech is the language. The written record is but a secondary representation of language.' (2) Language is a system of forms. The role of the linguist was to build up a description of this system. (3) The language system is arbitrary. (4) Language is for communication. The structuralists never developed this promising axiom except to the extent that they collected the real data of speech from their informants.

The structuralist linguist adopted a strongly empirical and inductive approach to the description of language, *i.e.,* 'texts' — actual sound recordings or transcriptions — constituted the data which was then segmented into progressively small units. Structuralist descriptions are partial and fail to reveal the infinite capacity which language has for creating new sentences.

The structural linguist soon became involved in language teaching. The second world war in particular created the urgent need for teaching methods. The philosophical position adopted by the structuralists in relation to human learning was mechanist. The dichotomy between mind and body was denied. The activities of the mind were seen as no more complex extensions of the activities of the body. The psychology of the behaviourist school provided the model of learning accepted by the structuralists. Since language was a human activity it was believed that learning language was achieved by building up habits on the basis of stimulus-response chains. The way of building up these habits was to provide unremitting practice. Structuralist language teaching materials cover an enormous range of text books. Fries' preface to *English Sentence Patterns* (1957) stands on its own as a monument of structuralism as applied to language teaching.

Structuralist linguistics from the time of Saussure early in the century to that of Fries and Harris in the 1950s represented a major advance in the establishment of linguistics as an independent discipline.

Transformational-generative Linguistics

Transformational-generative linguistics (or grammar) was the result of a period of mounting dissatisfaction in the 1950s with structuralist linguistics. The first important publication was Chomsky's *Syntactic Structures* (1957). Applications to language teaching were slow in coming. The earliest were Roberts' course for Italian Secondary schools (1962) and Chomsky's own in 1969.

For the transformationalists, language is a system of knowledge made manifest in linguistic forms but innate and universal. Language is a system which relates meanings to substance. Language is a mental phenomenon. Language is innate. Language is universal in the sense that all normal children the world over acquire a mother tongue and all languages must share key characteristics.

The transformationalists have been cautious in applying their theory to actual classroom teaching. Language teachers and applied linguists have drawn out of TG a number of assumptions which have influenced language teaching. The philosophical position adopted by the transformationalists in relation to human learning is mentalistic. The dichotomy between body and mind has been reasserted. The activities of the mind are seen different from those of the body. Learning requires a philosophical rather than physiological or psychological explanation. The psychology of cognitive theorists provides a model for the learning or acquiring of language. Language is essentially a thinking process. Language learning can best be explained as a process of problem-solving in which the learner attempts to create cognitive maps for himself by means of which he makes sense of the data. He acts like a scientist formulating hypotheses about the system to which he is being exposed and trying the rules he has worked out on native speakers.

The way forward for applied linguistics in the 1960s and much more clearly in the 1970s, was to be through a new answer to the question 'What is language?' From this emerged a new approach — functionalism.

Functionalism

By functionalism we mean a view of language as a dynamic, open system by means of which members of a community exchange information. This is in contrast with the static, closed-system view of language which has been the commonly accepted orientation since Saussure (1915), seeing language as a code made up of elements and their relationships with each other.

There are three key problems which have important implications for linguistics proper as well as for applied linguistics : the place of semantics in grammar, the relationship of variation to the model and the problem of the function of the language. After Saussure linguistics tended to avoid the discussion of meaning, leaving it to the human sciences to describe, and to concentrate on the description of the syntactic and phonological level of the code. This was the policy of the structuralist linguistics. With TG there came a revived interest in semantics.

There are very many functionalist approaches which have been put forward. They are often very different from one another. Two prominent ones are Role-and-Reference Grammar (RRG), developed by William Foley and Robert Van Valin, and Systemic Linguistics (SL) developed by Michael Halliday. RRG approaches linguistic description by asking what communicative purposes need to be served and what grammatical devices are available to serve them. SL is chiefly interested in examining the structure of a large linguistic unit — a text or a discourse. It attempts to integrate a great deal of structural information with other information in the hope of constructing a coherent account of what speakers are doing.

Functionalist approaches have proved fruitful. But they are usually hard to formalize. They often work with "patterns," "preferences," "tendencies" and "choices" in place of the explicit rules preferred by non-functionalist linguists.

Phonetics

Phonetics is the study of speech sounds. Strictly speaking phonetics is not part of linguistics. Of course there are close connections between the two disciplines. Phoneticians investigate such topics as the anatomical, physiological and neurological basis of speech, the actions of the speech organs in producing speech sounds, the acoustic nature of the sound waves which transmit speech. Phoneticians may choose to investigate either the total range of speech sounds which can be produced by human beings, or the manner in which speech sounds are used in real human languages. Phonetics was substantially developed by the ancient Indians and by the medieval Arabs. The modern tradition began in the sixteenth century in English. It was in nineteenth and twentieth century Britain that such figures as Alexander Melville Bell, Henry Sweet and Daniel Jones chiefly created modern phonetics.

Phoneme

Phoneme is one of the basic sound units of a language. Every spoken languages possesses a smallest set of basic abstract sound units, both consonants and vowels, and every word in that language must consist of permitted sequence of those basic sound units called phonemes. The number of phonemes in particular languages varies considerably.

Phonology

Phonology is the sound system of languages, or the branch of linguistics which studies these. It deals with the ways in which sounds behave in languages. It is a central part of linguistics. It took a long time for the linguists to understand the difference between phonetics and phonology. Important contributions to phonology were made by the European linguists of the Prague School in the 1930s and by the American structuralists in the 1940s, and 1950s. In the late 1950s phonology was transformed by the introduction of distinctive features (phonological units smaller than phonemes).

These features were combined with certain ideas taken from Noam Chomsky's new theory of transformational grammar to produce a drammatically new approach named generative phonology which focused on the phonological processes occurring in languages.

Philology

Philology is the branch of historical linguistics concerned with the histories of individual words and names. Historical linguists exhibit a range of interests. Some are chiefly interested in determining which languages are connected in genetic relationships and in working out the structures of particular language families. Others are concerned with identifying the particular changes which have affected individual languages. Still others are looking for general principles of language change. But some are mainly interested in identifying the origins of particular words or names and in tracing the histories of these items through time. We give the name philology to this pursuit. We divide philology into etymology and onomastics. Philological work is exacting. It requires a mastery of detail perhaps greater than in any other branch of linguistics.

Etymology

Etymology is the origin and history of a particular word, or the branch of linguistics that studies this. Every language has a vocabulary containing many thousands of words, and everyone of those words has its own particular origin and history, *i.e.,* its own etymology. Specialists in etymology make it their business to uncover the origins of words, one by one. Doing this successfully requires a prodigious knowledge of the language containing the word being investigated and of any neighbouring or related languages from which the data may be relevant. It also requires the scrutiny of any number of old documents, sometimes very old documents, in order to extract every available scrap of information about the world.

Onomastics

Onomastics is the study of names. It is a branch of philology. Its pursuit requires the same painstaking scrutiny of historical documents as any other branch of philology. Onomasticians study both anthroponyms and toponyms.

Phonotactics

The rules for combining phonemes into words in a language are phonotactics. Every variety of every language possesses a larger or smaller set of phonemes. Every legitimate word in that language must consist of a permitted sequence of those phonemes. No language allows its phonemes to occur in any sequence at all. Instead, each language imposes strict limits on the sequences of phonemes which are allowed to occur in a word, these restrictions are its phonotactics.

Morpheme

Morpheme is the smallest identifiable grammatical unit. We sometimes think of words as the smallest units of grammar, but words in fact are not the smallest grammatical units. For example, the word 'unhappiness' is clearly built up from three smaller pieces : the prefix 'un-,' the stem 'happy' and the suffix '-ness.' Each of these piece is a morpheme of English, and not one of them can be broken down any further in grammatical terms : all of them are minimal units. Each of these morphemes is used to build other English words. For example, the prefix 'un-' occurs also in 'unhappy,' 'unclear,' 'unwilling' etc.; the stem 'happy' occurs in 'unhappy,' 'happiness,' 'happier,' 'happily' and of course in the word 'happy' itself; and the suffix '-ness' occurs in 'quickness,' 'sadness' etc.

Morphemes are of different types. We say that 'happy' is a lexical morpheme, meaning that it has dictionary meaning. But the '-ly,' of 'happily' is different. This is a grammatical morpheme which performs a strictly grammatical function. Quite independently 'happy' is a free morpheme. It can stand alone to make a word as it does in the word 'happy.' The prefix 'un-' and the suffixes '-ly,' and '-ness' are bound morphemes. They can never stand alone, but must always be attached to atleast one other morpheme within a word.

In the ideal case, a single morpheme has a single constant form and a single constant meaning or function. In practice, many morphemes vary in form, depending on where they occur. For example, the morpheme 'sane' has one form when it occurs in words 'sane' and 'insane;' but a different form in when it occurs in the word 'sanity.' We call these variant forms allomorphs. It was Bloomfield and his American successors who made the study of morphemes a central part of linguistics.

Morphology

Morphology is the branch of linguistics which studies word structure. Words typically have internal structure. They consist of smaller units called morphemes. Morphology is conventionally divided into two main areas. These are inflexion and word formation. Inflection refers to the variation in form of a single word for grammatical purposes as with 'take,' takes; 'took,' 'taken,' 'taking.' Word formation refers to the construction of new words from existing words as with 'textbook' from 'text' and 'book,' and with 'slowly' from 'slow' and '-ly.' A particularly different form of word formation is derivation.

Movement

Movement refers to any of various processes or structure in which an element of a sentence appears in a position other than its canonical position. Grammarians have long realized that some particular sentences depart from the usual norms in the order of their elements. It was only in the 1950s, originally within the formalism of transformational grammar, that linguists began to speak of the movement of elements out of their ordinary position. Movement phenomena are numerous and diverse. One familiar example in English involves question words (WH-words) referred to as WH-movement or extraction. Another type of movement is extraction in which a complex element is shifted to the end of its sentence. Yet another type of movement is fronting in which an element is moved to the beginning of its sentence. When an element is fronted to make it an explicit topic, we speak of topicalization.

Orthography

Orthography refers to a standard system for writing a particular language. A given orthography consists of a particular version of a particular writing system, a standardized system of spelling and a particular system of pronunciation. Often there are additional devices such as the use of arabic numerals for writing numbers, the specialized use of certain symbols, the presence of certain abbreviations, and the use of distinctive type faces like italic and bold face.

Semantics

Semantics is the branch of linguistics which studies meaning. The study of meaning has something of a chequered history in linguistics. People have since ancient times been interested in questions of meaning. But very little progress was made before the late nineteenth century. The French linguist Michel Breel coined the term semantics and introduced it into European linguistics. Once the Swiss linguist Ferdinand de Saussure had made linguistic sign the corner-stone of his influential theories, semantics was here to stay in European linguistics. American linguists were comparatively reluctant to consider semantic questions. Edward Sapir and Leonard Bloomfield did not entirely neglect the matter. Their successors the American structuralists of 1940s and 1950s were pessimistic about semantics. In the 1960s, shortly after the Chomskyan revolution, a few American linguists began to be interested in semantic questions. The work of the American philosopher Richard Montague had an enormous effect upon linguistics. Montague's ideas have become the basis of a great deal of important work in linguistic semantics. In recent years approaches to semantics have proliferated. The majority of the current approaches represent versions of formal semantics.

Word

Word is a linguistic unit typically larger than a morpheme but smaller than a phrase. The term 'word' might seem familiar and straightforward enough. In fact words can be defined in at least four different ways, and these ways are not equivalent at all. An orthographic word is something written with white spaces at both ends but no white space in the middle. Orthographic words are of minimal linguistic interest. A phonological word is something pronounced as a single unit. A lexical item or Lexeme is a dictionary word, an item which you could expect to find having its own entry in a dictionary. A grammatical word form or morphosyntactic word is any one of the several forms which a lexical item may assume for grammatical purposes. Consider the word 'icecream.' It is two orthographic words but a single phonological word, a single lexical item and a single grammatical word form. The contraction 'hasn't' is a single orthographic word and a single phonological word but it's two lexical items ('have' and 'not') and two grammatical word-forms ('has' and 'not'). The study of words is lexicology.

Sentence

Sentence is the largest purely grammatical unit in a language. There are larger linguistic units than sentences : individual paragraphs, individual turns and individual discourses. But these larger units are no more than very weakly linked by purely grammatical means. The largest linguistic unit which is held together by rigid grammatical rules is the sentence. For most linguists, in most circumstances, a sentence is an abstract linguistic object. A sentence is not just a string of words. It is a string of words with a grammatical structure assigned to it.

Syntax

Syntax is the branch of linguistics which studies sentence structure. The first European steps in the examination of syntax were taken by the Greeks beginning with Aristotle. In 1940s the American linguist Zellig Harris began developing an interesting new way of looking at syntax. A decade later his student Noam Chomsky presented a greatly modified version of Harris's ideas, involving the introduction generative grammar and of the peculiar variety of generative grammar called transformational generative grammar. Chomsky argued that syntax was not only tractable but the very heart of serious linguistic investigation. He persuaded a generation of linguists that he was correct. As a result the study of syntax became vastly more prominent. In 1960s the American linguist Joseph Greenberg published his pioneering work in syntactic typology.

4

Linguistic Dichotomies

Speech and Writing

Linguistics has developed with considerable vigour. It has become an autonomous academic discipline. The focusing on spoken rather than written language has brought additional data within the range of linguistic study. This range has been extended in other directions by contact with sociology and psychology. So diverse are the developments in language study that the boundaries of linguistic science are impossible to define.

Linguistics is not about language teaching. Both linguistics and language teaching have language as their subject matter. Each can learn something from the other. Linguistics does have implications for language teaching. These implications must be used to evaluate language teaching practices. Linguistics is one of the fields to which language teaching may be referable.

Linguistics has brought to the study of language a revaluation of the relationship between the spoken and written forms of the language. Traditionally in the description of the languages a much higher status was accorded to the written than to the spoken. The written language is the repository of the finest literary achievements of a society. If one wishes to discover what is 'finest,' what is 'most beautiful,' what is quite simply the 'best,' it is to the written literature that one looks Speech is transitory. In the past there was no means of seizing it, of relieving speech events, and of making them available to others. Written language is held up as a norm for all our uses of language. The linguistic attitude attaches the greater importance to speech. For the linguist speech is the primary manifestation of language; writing is both secondary to it and dependent on it.

It is part of man's biological nature that he should speak, just as it is that he should walk. Men do not necessarily learn to write. There are many societies where writing is unknown. With physiological, neurological and psychological normality, a child will talk. Every individual learns to speak before he learns to write. Languages change and the most potent force of change is speech. Sound systems seem to be permanently in a state of flux and grammatical systems are not completely stable either. Where change has occurred in speech, the written language may eventually be changed to accommodate it.

The linguist has speech as his main subject matter. He would not dismiss written language from his field of study. The primacy of speech is of some importance to the language teacher. The linguist's interest in language is in attempting to describe the very complex structure that is the ultimate goal of the learner. Social and personal factors enter into the definition of the goals of language teaching.

Spoken language now has a status in education which it did not previously possess. In the teaching of both the mother-tongue and foreign languages, the principal goal has been proficiency in the written forms. Now there is a realization that the improvement of skill in spoken expression and understanding is a legitimate goal of language teaching.

Form and Meaning

Linguistics makes a clear distinction between statements about the use of which we put language (its meaning) and the actual shape which units of language and the relationship which exists between them (its form). It is the function of linguistic forms to convey meaning. Scholars have been studying language for more than two thousand years. They have adopted varied views on which aspect of language most deserved their attention. Some have assumed that whatever language we speak, a universal conceptual system underlies our use of that language. Others have believed that far from there being a universal system of grammar, every language should be examined with a minimum of preconceptions and its regularities explained only on the basis of observable evidence. For every language there would be different descriptive framework.

Statements about language should be based on evidence that is available to all. Only in this way could linguistics be an objective scientific study. It is sometimes said that a statement is only worth making if it is clear by what means we might attempt to deprove it. The forms of language can be studied in this way.

Meaning is not susceptible to such an approach. Evidence of the meaning of language is not available to all. The meaning of items of language is compounded of the internal states of both speakers and hearers, of the physical and linguistic context in which the language is produced, of the biographical experience of the individuals concerned in the language event and so on. Linguists have felt that it is impossible to make precise statements about meaning.

It is with the dominance of form in the form/meaning dichotomy that linguistics has until recently been most associated. Language teaching should be based on a full understanding of both the formal and semantic nature of language.

Substance and Form

Sounds and symbols such as letters of the alphabet that represent sounds in writing are the raw material of language. They are the phonic (sound) and graphic (written) substances of the language. In themselves, they have no meaning. It is only when they are given a particular shape or order that they become meaningful. That is, it is only when they have some form that they have meaning.

All distinct sounds produced by human speech organs and written scripts are the substance of human language. A cluster of sounds such as /n/, /t/, /f/ etc. is only noise. It has no meaning. It must be suitably arranged into some form to make it meaningful.

Substance and form are two parts of the quality of language. Substance, which is the mere sound or word, is only the 'signifier' in Saussure's terms. In order to make it sense, it has to be linked with the 'signified,' that is the meaning or the concept. Form includes both grammar and semantics.

We can say that substance is the element or raw material of language. Form is the associative order in which the raw materials are brought together in a meaningful way. Form is the concern of linguistic study. It is form that makes it possible to study substance.

Sign and Symbol

The language system is made up of signs. Sign is the central fact of language. A sign is a physical marker which carries some information. The information it gives is direct, brief and precise. This is opposed to symbol which means more than mere indication. It contains more information. It stands in place of something as a means of pointing towards it indirectly. For example, the gesture of waving one's hand is a sign but can be interpreted variously as symbolic of farewell, dismissal etc. Similarly a way of dressing or eating is a sign which signals some social practice or belief. This concept when applied to all our behaviour and to our society and culture shows us that our entire culture is made up of signs which are of special significance. Saussure's notion of sign has led to the growth of a whole area of study of the operation of signs in culture and society called semiotics.

The linguistic sign consists of two parts. The signifier and the signified, or the word which signifies and the object that is signified as

Tree signifies.

But the word 'tree' does not signify the actual object, *i.e.,* the tee. If it did, the word for this object in all languages would have been the same *i.e.,* 'tree.' But we know that this object is called by different names in different languages. This means that the word 'tree' does not represent the actual object in real life. It represents the concept or the image of the object that we have in our minds. We invent a word consisting of some sound-images which we then use to represent the concept that exists in our minds. There is no logical reason why we choose certain combination of sounds to represent the concept. So we say that the relationship between sounds and words and the concept they signify is an arbitrary one.

We can modify the earlier diagram regarding sign in the following manner :

Tree ———→ signifies ———→ concept of tree
(sound/word image-signifier) (mental image = signified)

That which signifies (the word) is the signifier. That which is signified (the object) is the signified. Sign is the composite of both. It consists of a relationship between the signifier and the signified. This relationship, once established, continues over a long period of time. It is established as a social fact *i.e.* by society.

Many such signs make up the system of a language. Signs are relational entities. They exist only in terms of relation to each other. They enter into complex relations with each other. These relationships constitute the whole system of the language. Signs differ from one language to another. Concepts about the signified differ from one language to another. Every society constitutes its own concepts of the real world and links these concepts to certain signifiers and signifieds. Once the relationships are made individuals are not free to choose any arbitrary signifiers they want to choose.

A symbol is a kind of sign that signifies several concepts on the basis of the primary relationship between signifier and signified. That is, the word 'tree' signifies the concept of tree. This is the primary relationship. It may also signify 'life,' 'growth,' 'nature' etc. When it does, it becomes not only a sign but also a symbol. It follows that a symbol is built up of several associative relationships between signifiers and the signifieds. That is why we say that language is a system of symbolic signs.

Structure-System Dichotomy

(Syntagmatic and paradigmatic relationships)
(The duality of Structure)

We say that language is structured and that it is a system of systems. It is structured in such a way that its elements are inter-related to form a system at each level of its structure. Thus, sounds are inter-related to form the phonological system, words are inter-related to form the morphological system and word classes are inter-related to form the syntactic system.

To give an example of this Robins compares the structure of language to that of an orchestra. The members of an orchestra are all related to each other by their specific roles as orchestra players in the orchestra as a whole and as smaller groups within the orchestra. Each performs his function by virtue of his place in relation to the others. Players can not be added to or taken away from an orchestra without changing its quality. That is what we mean by structure : an ordered competition of many parts, each part being related to the whole, and also related to other elements within it. Each part, by inter-relationship of elements in it, constitutes a system.

Within each system, elements are selected and combined in building up the structure. For example, if we wish to build up a word such as 'take,' we will select some sounds and combine them in a particular order. In the process of selection, certain rules operate. We can select one element at a time from among a class of similar elements : *e.g.,* a particular consonant from a class of similar consonants; a noun from a class of nouns. With reference to the above example, we choose the consonant /t/ instead of /k/ or /b/ which we would have chosen because they are all plosives.

The relation between a set of linguistic items which constitute choices so that only one of them may be present at a time in a given position is referred to as paradigmatic relation. Paradigmatic relationship holds between several elements that belong to the same class within a system. The notion of paradigmatic relation was introduced by Saussure as a generalization of the traditional concept of a paradigm. What Saussure did was to point out that the relation among the several forms in a traditional paradigm is essentially the same as the relation among other sets of linguistic elements. For example, the English determiners a/an, some, the, this/these and that/those, all stand in a paradigmatic relation, because, in a single noun phrase, there will be one and only one of them at the beginning : *e.g.,* a book, some books, the book and so on.

In the process of combination of the elements we combine the chosen elements in a particular order or sequence. Here too there are certain rules. For example, we can combine /t/ + /ei/ + /k/ in this order, but not in the order /ei/ + /t/ + /k/. The three elements that follow one another in a particular sequence are related in what can be called a syntagmatic relationship. One follows the other in linear order. It is by following this order that the structure of a word or a sentence is built up. Thus

Paradigmatic relationship	=	between elements in a class or system; only one can operate at a time.
Syntagmatic relationship	=	between elements in a linear sequence

To illustrate with an example

↕ paradigmatic (vertical)					
	l	t	ei	k →	
	l	b	ei	k →	syntagmatic
	l	t	u	k →	(horizontal/linear)
	l	b	ei	t →	

In the paradigmatic relationship /t/ can be replaced by /b/, /ei/ can be replaced by /u/, /k/ can be replaced by /t/. Each can be replaced by another element from within the same system and class. So, in the above example, we cannot put a consonant in place of the vowel by another. In the syntagmatic relationship, the elements have to be combined in the proper sequence. We cannot violate the sequential order. On the basis of these paradigmatic and syntagmatic relationships, rules of selection and combination operate. Taken together, these constitute the structure of a language. They are like the two intersecting threads that build up the fabric of a language. Because of these relationships we say that language has duality of structure. At one level, we select particular elements out of many, at another level, we combine these elements to form a structural unit.

The concept of syntagmatic relation was introduced by Saussure. In his terminology any kind of structural unit in a language at any level is a syntagm or syntagma. A syntagm consists of some set of smaller structural units. For example, the English phonemes /t/, /k/ and /æ/ are syntagmatically related in one way in /tæk/ tack, in a second way in /kæt/ cat, in a third way in /æ kt/ act; and in a fourth way in /tækt/ tact. Similarly, the morphemes {un-}, {happy} and {-ness} are syntagmatically related in a particular way in the word 'unhappiness.' The words 'the,' 'little' and 'girl' are syntagmatically related in the noun phrase 'the little girl'. A particular pattern into which a large number of individual syntagms fit in is a structure. Today, we more usually apply the term 'structure' to each particular instance of a general pattern, and avoid the term 'syntagm.'

To sum up, system is the set of paradigmatic relationships between elements. Structure is the set of syntagmatic relationships between elements at each level in the language. At the level of sounds there is a phonological system consisting of vowels and consonants and a phonological structure determining the combination of these vowels and consonants. At the level of sentence formation there is a syntactic system consisting of word classes and a syntactic structure to enable the formation of sentences.

Note that in psycholinguistics the term 'paradigmatic relation' is used to denote the mental associations between words; syntagmatic relations denote the mental association between words which frequently occur together.

Diachronic and Synchronic Approaches

The distinction between substance and form is made in linguistics between two approaches to the study of language. The synchronic approach sees language as a living whole, existing as a 'state,' at one particular time. This 'state' of language is an accumulation of all the linguistic activities that a language community engages in during a specified period. To study language, linguists can collect sample of this language as it exists, describe them regardless of any historical considerations. Once linguists have isolated a focal point for synchronic description, the time factor becomes irrelevant.

The diachronic approach traces the historical development of the language. If records the changes that have taken place in it between successive points in time. *Diachronic* is therefore equivalent to 'historical.' The diachronic approach investigates language changes and the evolution of languages.

Saussure made the distinction between the two approaches. He gives priority in linguistics to the synchronic approach. He observes that the two approaches should be kept separate. He has given the inter-relationship of diachrony and synchrony in this way.

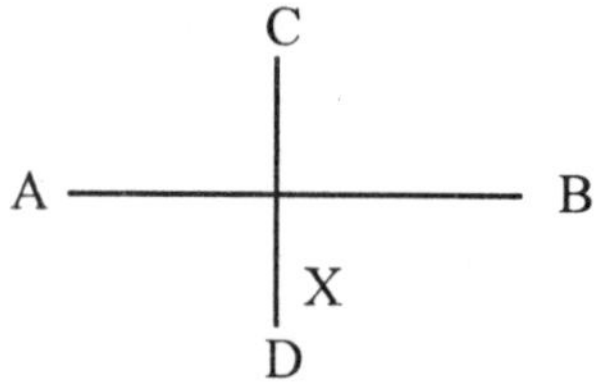

In the diagram AB is the synchronic axis of simultaneities, *i.e.*, all the facts of languages as they co-exist at a particular time. It is the static axis. CD is the diachronic axis of successions. That is, CD is an imaginary line moving through time, the historical path through which language has travelled and will continue travelling. AB can intersect CD at any point. X is the point in CD where the particular point in time can be isolated and the language as it exists at that point can be described.

The priority of synchronic over diachronic study is explained by Saussure by analogy with the game of chess. The chessboard is constantly changing during the game, as each player makes his move. But, if someone enters into the room at any moment during the game, he can understand the state of the game by looking at the positions occupied by the pieces. It does not matter how many moves, or what kind of moves have been made before arriving at that stage in the game. The rules that are agreed upon, before the game begins, continue to operate with each move. Similar rules exist in language too. To pass from one stage to the next, only one piece needs to be moved at a time. Thus in language, change effects only isolated elements. Of course these stages do ultimately result in changing the language, just as a succession of moves can change the outcome of the game.

Language can and should be described synchronically, in its own terms without reference to what it has developed from, or what it is likely to develop into. This does not mean that diachronic or historical study cannot be done. To give historical studies a better and more valid base, good synchronic study is essential.

Langue and Parole

Modern linguistics is based on some fundamental concepts which are expounded by linguists in the beginning of the twentieth century. The most influential of these were Bloomfield, Chomsky and Saussure. The main ideas regarding language propounded by these linguists take the form of certain distinctions or dichotomies by means of which we are able to understand the nature of language in a more systematic and complete way.

Saussure made a distinction between two aspects of language : 'Langue' and 'Parole.' 'Langue' means language, that is all the rules and conventions regarding the combination of sounds, formation of words and sentences, pronunciation and meaning. There is a similarity of sounds, words and meaning among the native speakers of a language. It means that they have the same images and signs in their minds. As Saussure puts it : 'If we embrace the sum of word images stored in the mind of all individuals we could identify the social bond that constitutes language. It is a storehouse filled by the members of a given community through their active use, a grammatical system that has a potential existence in each brain, or more specifically in the brains, of a group of individuals. For language is not complete in any speaker; it exists perfectly only within a collectivity.'

It follows that language is social, a set of conventions shared by all the speakers of a language. Language is abstract, as these particular conventions exist in the minds of the speakers who belong to that society that has created the language.

'Parole' belongs to the individual. When those conventions that exist in the mind as 'langue' are used in a concrete form in actual speech or writing, they become instances of 'parole.' 'Parole' is the actual sounds and sentences produced by an individual speaker or writer. It is a concrete physical manifestation of the abstract 'langue' that exists in the mind. If we hear a person speaking a language that we do not know, we hear the sounds and sentences, that is the 'parole.' We cannot understand them because we do not share the conventions or 'langue' that are behind the individual sounds and sentences. So 'langue' is the underlying system which makes the individual performance or 'parole' meaningful.

'Parole' is individual performance in speech or writing. It is concrete and physical. It makes use of the psychological mechanism in uttering words and sentences. 'Langue' exists in the mind of each individual in the form of word images and knowledge of conventions as an abstract form of grammar and dictionary of the language. An individual makes use of this knowledge in his or her own way to produce actual sentences, that is 'parole.' Individuals can communicate with each other because they share the same 'langue.' But they produce different sentences based on the same 'langue.' Their production of sentences is marked as being variable, unpredictable, heterogeneous, inventive and whimsical. It can be said that the language system is 'langue,' while language behaviour is 'parole.'

Saussure considered 'langue' as the legislative side of language, or the law of the language. Like law, 'langue' maintains the social order and homogeneity of the language. 'Parole' is the executive side of the language. It uses the law or code of the language (langue) for its individual ends. It executes 'langue' through individual acts of speaking and writing.

The dichotomy between 'langue' and 'parole' is made by the analogy of a game of chess. In the game the rules are determined and they are understood by all the players, but each game is different and depends on the individual performances which differ from player to player.

According to Saussure we can only study 'langue' and not 'parole.' 'Langue' is a well-defined, homogeneous object distinct from the heterogeneous unpredictable mass of speech acts. 'Langue' consists of signs which bear the stamp of collective approval. The signs can be converted into conventional written symbols and so they can be studied. Individual acts of speaking cannot be accurately represented. They are so variable that they cannot be studied.

Competence and Performance

There is a complex and changing relationship between the language and situational and personal features. No one act of language is ever quite like another. The act of speech is distinguished by much that is the product of our personality, our temperament, or our physical incapacities and by those distortions in our speech which are not part of the system of the language. Saussure has termed and explained the dichotomy as 'langue' and 'parole.' The American linguist Noam Chomsky uses the terms 'competence' (langue) and 'performance' (parole).

'Competence,' according to Chomsky, is the native speaker's knowledge of his language, the mastery of the system of rules. 'Performance' is the production of actual sentences in use in real life situations. So a speaker's knowledge of the structure of the language is the speaker's linguistic competence. The way in which he uses it is linguistic performance.

Competence is a set of principles which a speaker masters. Performance is what a speaker does. Competence is a kind of code. Performance is the act of encoding or decoding. Competence is free from interference due to slips of memory, lapses of attention etc. Performance reflects many such lapses. Competence is ideal. It gives us a coherent picture of the language. It can be studied. It is difficult to get a direct, coherent record of performance.

Chomsky's concept of competence and performance closely resembles Saussure's langue-parole dichotomy. But it differs in that while langue is the same with every language user, competence may differ from person to person. Saussure's understanding of langue emphasises its predominantly social aspect. Chomsky's term 'competence' is based on psychology and presumes individual differences between human beings. Thus speaker A may be more competent than speaker B, though they may share the same conventions of the language. Similarly A's performance would also be different from that of B. Chomsky's view of competence is also based on the idea of an inbuilt language acquisition device in humans that enables a person to acquire competence.

Competence is our ability to use language. When we use our language, we commit all sorts of errors. We make slips of the tongue, we sometimes cannot think of a word or name we know perfectly well, we interrupt ourselves, we mishear or misunderstand what others are saying, we may even lose the thread of what we ourselves are saying, there are limits to our memories, and so on. Chomsky argues that such errors should be dismissed from consideration in examining our ability to use the language. According to him everyone of us possess an abstract linguistic competence which is independent of the errors we sometimes make. Chomsky wants this competence to be the principal business of linguistic theory.

Some socio-linguists regard the dichotomies as unreal. Langue and parole are inter-related and not separate. Parole can also be studied. We cannot keep parole or performance out of our study of language because it gives us useful insight into language processes. It is now easier to study performance through audio-video devices. The distinction is still useful.

5

Teaching Methodology

It has been estimated that more than sixty percent of today's world population is bilingual. Both from a contemporary and a historical perspective, bilingualism or multilingualism is the norm. It is fair to say that foreign language learning has always been an important practical concern. Whereas today English is the world's most widely studied foreign language, five hundred years ago it was Latin. By the nineteenth century the approach based on the study of Latin had become the standard way of studying foreign languages in schools. A typical text in the mid-nineteenth century consisted of chapters or lessons organized around grammar points. Each grammar point was listed, rules on its use were explained, and it was illustrated by sample sentences. Nineteenth century text book compilers were mainly determined to codify the foreign language into frozen rules of morphology and syntax to be explained and eventually memorized. Oral work was reduced to an absolute minimum. A handful of written exercises came as a sort of appendix to the rules. This approach to foreign language teaching became known as Grammar-Translation Method.

Grammar-Translation Method

Grammar translation was the offspring of German scholarship. Its object was to know everything about something rather than the thing itself. It was first known in the US as the Prussian method. The principal characteristics of the Grammar-Translation method were these :

(1) The goal of foreign language study is to learn a language in order to read its literature, or in order to benefit from the mental discipline and intellectual development. Grammar-

Translation is a way of studying a language that approaches the language first through detailed analysis of its grammar rules, followed by the application of this knowledge to the task of translating sentences and texts into and out of the target language. It views language learning as consisting of little more than memorizing rules and facts in order to understand and manipulate the morphology and syntax of the foreign language. The first language is maintained as the reference system in the acquisition of the second language.

(2) Reading and writing are the major focus. Little or no systematic attention is paid to speaking or listening.

(3) Vocabulary selection is based solely on the reading texts used. Words are taught through bilingual word-lists, dictionary study and memorization.

(4) The sentence is the basic unit of teaching. Much of the lesson is devoted to translating sentences into and out of the target language. It is this focus on the sentence is the distinctive feature of the method.

(5) Accuracy is emphasized. Students are expected to attain high standards in translation.

(6) Grammar is taught deductively, that is by presentation and study of grammar rules which are then practised through translation exercises.

(7) The student's native language is the medium of instruction.

Grammar-Translation method dominated European and foreign language teaching from the 1840s to the 1940s. In modified form it continues to be widely used in some parts of the world today.

Although the method often creates frustration for students, it makes few demands on teachers. It is still used in situations where understanding literary text is the primary focus of foreign language study. Contemporary texts for the teaching of foreign language at college level often reflect Grammar-Translation principles. These texts are frequently the products of people trained in literature rather than in language teaching or applied linguistics. In the mid and late nineteenth century opposition to Grammar-Translation method gradually developed in several European countries. This Reform Movement, as it was referred to, laid the foundations for the development of new ways of teaching language and raised controversies that have continued the present day.

Reform Movement in Language Teaching

Towards the mid nineteenth century several factors contributed to a questioning and rejection of Grammar-Translation Method. Increased opportunities for communication created a demand for oral proficiency in foreign languages.

Gouin a French man developed an approach to teaching a foreign language based on his observations of children's use of language. He believed that language learning was facilitated through using language to accomplish events consisting of a sequence of related actions. His method used situations and themes as ways of organizing and presenting oral language. Gouin established schools to teach according to his method; and it was quite popular for a time. Gouin's emphasis on the need to present new teaching items in a context that makes their meaning clear, and the use of gestures and actions to convey the meaning of utterances are practices that later became part of such approaches and methods as situational language Teaching and Total Physical Response.

Educators recognized the need for speaking proficiency rather than reading comprehension, grammar or literary appreciation as the goal for foreign language programmes. There was an interest in how children learn their languages. From 1880s practically minded linguists like Henry Sweet in England, Wilhelm Victor in Germany and Paul Passy in France began to provide the intellectual leadership needed to give reformist ideas greater credibility and acceptance. The discipline of linguistics was revitalized. Phonetics was established giving new insights into speech processes. Linguists emphasized that speech was the primary form of language. The International Phonetic Association was formed in 1886 and its International Phonetic Alphabet (IPA) was designed to enable the sounds of any language to be accurately transcribed.

Reform Movement advocated :

(1) the study of the spoken language;

(2) phonetic training in order to establish good pronunciation habits;

(3) the use of conversation texts and dialogues to introduce conversational phrases and idioms;

(4) an inductive approach to the teaching of grammar;

(5) teaching new meanings through establishing associations within the target language.

Linguists became interested in the controversies that emerged about the best way to teach foreign languages. Ideas were fiercely discussed and defended in books, articles and pamphlets. Henry Sweet argued that second methodological principles should be based on a scientific analysis of language and study of psychology. Victor in Germany used linguistic theory to justify his views on language teaching. He argued that training in phonetics would enable teachers to pronounce the language correctly. Speech patterns were the fundamental elements of language. None of the proposals of the reformists assumed the status of a method. This led to what have been termed 'Natural methods' and ultimately the Direct Method.

The Direct Method

Throughout the history of language teaching, attempts have been made to make second language learning more like first language. Sauveur used intensive oral interaction in the target language, employing questions as a way of presenting and eliciting language. He opened a language school in Boston in the late 1860s. His method soon became referred to as the Natural Method.

Sauveur and other believers in the Natural Method argued that a foreign language could be taught without translation or the use of the learner's native tongue. The German scholar Franke wrote on the psychological principles of direct association between forms and meanings in the target language. He provided a theoretical justification for a monolingual approach to teaching. According to him a language could best be taught by using it actively in the class room. Teachers must encourage direct and spontaneous use of the foreign language in the classroom. Learners would then be able to induce rules of grammar. The teacher replaced the textbook in the early stages of learning. Speaking began with systematic attention to pronunciation. Known words could be used to teach new vocabulary, using mime, demonstration and pictures. These natural language learning principles provided the foundation for what came to be known as the Direct Method.

Enthusiastic supporters of the Direct Method introduced it in France and Germany. It became widely known in the US through its use by Sauveur and Maximilian Berlitz in successful commercial language schools. (Berlitz never used the term; he referred to the method used in his schools as the Berlitz method.) In practice it stood for the following principles and procedures :

(1) Class room instruction was conducted exclusively in the target language.

(2) Only every vocabulary and sentences were taught.

(3) Oral communication skills were built up in a carefully graded programme organized around question-and-answer exchange, between teachers and students in small intensive classes.

(4) Grammar was taught inductively.

(5) New teaching points were introduced orally.

(6) Concrete vocabulary was taught through demonstration objects and pictures; abstract vocabulary was taught by association of ideas.

(7) Both speech and listening comprehension were taught.

(8) Correct pronunciation and grammar were emphasized.

The Direct Method was quite successful in private language schools. But it was difficult to implement in public secondary school education. It overemphasized and distorted the similarities between naturalistic first language learning and classroom foreign language learning. It failed to consider the practical realities of the classroom. It lacked a rigorous basis in applied linguistic theory.

The Direct Method represented the product of enlightened amateurism. It required teachers who were native speakers or who had native-like fluency in the foreign language. It was largely dependent on the teacher's skill, rather than on a text book. Henry Sweet viewed that it offered innovations at the level of teaching procedures but lacked a thorough methodological basis. Its main focus was on the exclusive use of the target language in the classroom. Sweet and others argued for the development of sound methodological principles that could serve as the basis for teaching techniques. In the 1920s and 1930s applied linguists systematized the principles proposed earlier by the Reform movement. Subsequent developments led to Audiolingualism in the US and the Oral Approach or Situational Language Teaching in Britain.

The Oral Approach and Situational Language Teaching

Few language teachers are familiar with the terms 'Oral Approach', or 'Situational Language Teaching'. They refer to an approach to language teaching developed by British applied linguists from 1930s to 1960s. Eventhough, neither term is commonly used today, the impact of Oral Approach has been long lasting.

Palmer, Hornby and other linguists developed an approach to methodology that involved systematic principles of selection, gradation and presentation. The linguists had differing views on the specific procedures to be used in teaching English. Their general principles were referred to as the Oral Approach to language teaching. This was not to be confused with the Direct Method which lacked a systematic basis in applied linguistic theory and practice.

The main characteristics of the approach were as follows : (1) Language teaching begins with the spoken language. Material is taught orally before it is presented in written form. (2) The target language is the language of the classroom. (3) New language points are introduced and practised situationally. (4) Vocabulary selection procedures are followed to ensure that an essential general service vocabulary is covered. (5) Items of grammar are graded following the principle that simple forms should be taught before complex ones. (6) Reading and writing are introduced once a sufficient lexical basis is established. It was the third principle that became a key feature of the approach in the sixties. It was then that the term 'situational' was used in referring to the approach.

The theory of language underlying SLT can be characterized as a type of British "structuralism." Speech was regarded as the basis of language. Structure was viewed as being at the heart of speaking ability. The theory that knowledge of structures must be linked to situations gave SLT one of its distinctive features. J.R. Firth and M.A.K. Halliday developed powerful views of language in which meaning, context and situation were given a prominent place.

The theory of learning underlying SLT is a type of behaviourist 'habit-learning' theory. It addresses primarily the processes rather than the conditions of meaning. SLT adopts an inductive approach to the teaching of grammar. The meaning of words or structures is to be induced from the way the form is used in a situation. Explanation is discouraged. The learner is expected to deduce the meaning of a particular structure or vocabulary item from the situation in which it is presented. The learner is expected to apply the language learned in a classroom to situations outside the classroom. The same processes are thought to occur in second and foreign language learning.

The objectives of SLT are to teach a practical command of the four basic skills of language. But the skills are approached through structure. Accuracy in pronunciation and grammar is regarded as crucial. Errors are to be avoided at all costs.

Basic to the teaching of English in SLT is a structured syllabus and a word list. Structures are taught within sentences. Vocabulary is chosen according to how well it enables sentence patterns to be taught. SLT employs a situational approach to presenting new sentence patterns and a drill-based manner of practising them. The practice techniques employed generally consist of guided repetition and substitution activities, including chorus repetitions, dictation, drills and controlled oral-based reading and writing tasks.

In the initial stages of learning, the learner is required, simply to listen and repeat what the teacher says and to respond to questions and commands. The learner has no control over the content of learning. Incorrect habits are to be avoided at all costs. Later, more active participation is encouraged.

The teacher's function is threefold. The teacher serves as a model, setting up situations. He becomes more like the conductor of an orchestra, drawing the music out of the performers. He is a skilful manipulator, using questions, commands to elicit correct sentences from the learners. Lessons are thus teacher-directed, and the teacher sets the pace.

SLT is depended upon both a textbook and visual aids. The textbook contains tightly organized lessons, planned around different grammatical structures. Visual aids may be produced by the teacher, or may be commercially produced. They consist of wall charts, flashcards, pictures and so on. In principle the textbook should be used only as a guide to the learning process. The teacher is expected to be the master of the textbook.

Classroom procedures vary according to the levels of the class. Procedures at any level aim to move from controlled to freer practice of structures and from oral use of sentence patterns to their automatic use in speech, reading and writing.

The Audio-Lingual Method

The Coleman Report in 1929 recommended a reading-based approach to foreign language teaching for use in American schools and colleges. This emphasized teaching the comprehension of texts. Teachers taught from books containing short reading passages in the foreign language, preceded by lists of vocabulary. Rapid silent reading was the goal. In practice teachers often resorted to discussing content of the passage in English. Those involved in the teaching of English as a second language in the U.S. between the two world wars used either a modified Direct Method approach, a reading-based approach or a reading-oral approach. There was little attempt to treat language content systematically. Sentence patterns and grammar were introduced at the whim of the textbook writer. There was no standardization of vocabulary or grammar that was included. The entry of the U.S. into the second World War had a significant effect on language teaching in America. The Government commissioned American Universities to develop foreign language programmes for military personal. Thus the Army Specialised Training Programme (ASTP) was established in 1942. Fiftyfive American universities were involved in the programme by the beginning of 1943.

The object of the army programmes was for students to attain conversational proficiency in a variety of foreign languages. The programme lasted only about two years. It attracted attention. For the next ten years the "Army Method" was discussed. In 1939 the University of Michigan developed the first English language institute of the U.S. It specialized in the training of teachers of English as a foreign language and in teaching English as a second or foreign language. Charles Fries, director of the Institute, was trained in structural linguistics. He applied the principles of structural linguistics to language teaching. For Fries grammar or structure was the starting point. The structure of the language was identified with its basic sentence patterns and grammatical structures. The language was taught with systematic attention to pronunciation and by intensive oral drilling of its basic sentence patterns. Pattern practice was a basic classroom technique. It is these basic patterns that constitute the learner's task. They require drill, drill and more drill, and only enough vocabulary to make such drills possible. US linguists were becoming increasingly active both within the US and abroad in supervising programmes for teaching English.

In many ways, the methodology used by the US linguists and language teaching experts at this period sounded similar to the British Oral Approach. The American approach differed in its strong alliance with American structural linguistics and its applied linguistic applications. Fries set forth his principles in *Teaching and Learning English as a Foreign Language* (1945). The approach developed by linguists at Michigan and other Universities became known variously as the Oral Approach, the Aural-oral approach, and the Structural Approach. It advocated aural training first, then pronunciation training followed by speaking, reading and writing. Language was identified with speech. Speech was approached through structures. It was the incorporation of the linguistic principles of the Aural-oral Approach with state-of-the-art psychological learning theory in the mid fifties that led to the method that came to be known as audiolingualism. The term was coined by Professor Nelson Brooks in 1964.

The theory of language underlying audiolingualism was derived from a view proposed by American linguists in the 1950s — a view that came to be known as structural linguistics. Language was viewed as a system of structurally related elements for the encoding of meaning, the elements being phonemes, morphemes, words, structures and sentence types.

In audiolingualism foreign language learning is a process of mechanical habit formation. Good habits are formed by giving correct responses. By memorizing dialogues and performing pattern drills, the chances of producing mistakes are minimized. Language is verbal behaviour. Aural-oral training is required to provide the foundation for the development of language skills. Analogy provides a better foundation for language learning than analysis. Analogy involves the process of generalizations and discriminations. Grammar is taught inductively. Vocabulary is introduced in a linguistic and cultural context.

Audiolingualists demanded a complete reorientation of the foreign language curriculum. They advocated a return to speech-based instruction with the primary object of oral proficiency. The teacher's role is central and active. It is a teacher-dominated method. The teacher models the target language, controls the direction, and pace of learning and monitors and corrects the learner's performance. The teacher must keep the learners attentive by varying drills and tasks and choosing relevant situations to practise structures. Language learning is seen to result from active verbal interaction between the teacher and the learner.

Audio-visual aids in audiolingual method assist the teacher to develop language mastery in the learner. They are primarily teacher-oriented. Tape-recorders and audio-visual equipment often have central roles. A language laboratory may also be considered essential. It provides the opportunity for further drill work and to receive controlled error-free practice of basic structures.

In a typical audiolingual lesson students first hear a model dialogue either read by the teacher or on tape containing the key structures that are the focus of the lesson. They repeat each line of the dialogue individually and in chorus. The teacher pays attention to pronunciation, intonation and fluency. Correction of mistakes is direct and immediate. The dialogue is memorized gradually, line by line. A line may be broken down into several phrases if necessary. The dialogue is read aloud in chorus. Then the dialogue is adapted to the learner's interest or situation through changing certain key words or phrases. Certain key structures from the dialogue are selected and used as the basis for pattern drills of different kinds. These are first practised in chorus and then individually. The learners may refer to their text book, and follow up reading, writing or vocabulary activities based on the dialogue may be introduced. Further activities may take place in the language laboratory.

The theoretical foundations of audiolingualism were attacked as being unsound both in terms of language theory and learning theory. Practitioners found that the practical results fell short of expectations. Students were often found to be unable to transfer skills acquired through audiolingualism to real communication outside the classroom. Many found the experience of study through audiolingual procedures boring and unsatisfying. Chomsky's theory of transformational grammar was to revolutionise American linguistics. Chomsky proposed an alternate theory of language learning to that of the behaviourists. To him much of the human language use is not imitated behaviour but is created anew form underlying knowledge of abstract rules. Sentences are not learned by imitation and repetition but 'generated from the learners' underlying "competence." The lack of an alternative to audiolingualism in language teaching in the US led to a period of adaptation, innovation and experimentation and some confusion.

Communicative Language Teaching

The origins of Communicative Language Teaching (CLT) are to be found in the changes in the British language teaching tradition dating from the late 1960s. Until then situational Language Teaching represented the major British approach to teaching English as a foreign language. British linguists saw the need to focus in language teaching a communicative proficiency rather than a mere mastery of structures. Scholars such as Candlin and Widdowson, drew on the works of British functional linguist John Firth, M.A.K. Halliday, American work on sociolinguists as well as work in philosophy.

In 1971 a group of experts began to investigate the possibility of developing language course on a unit-credit system. It is a system in which learning tasks are broken down into 'portions or units, each of which corresponds to a component of a learner's needs and is systematically related to all other portions.' The British linguist D.A. Wilkins proposed a functional or communicative definition of language that could serve as a basis for developing communicative syllabus for language teaching.

The work of the Council of Europe, the writings of Wilkins, Widdowson, Candlin, Brumfit, Keith Johnson and other British linguists on the theoretical basis for a communicative or functional approach to language teaching, the rapid application of these ideas by textbook writers and the rapid acceptance of these principles by British language teaching specialists came to be referred to as Communicative Language Teaching. The terms 'notional functional approach' and 'functional approach' are also sometimes used. Since the mid 1970s the scope of CLT has expanded. Both American and British proponents now see it as an approach that aims to make communicative competence the goal of language teaching. There is no single text or authority on it nor any single model that is universally accepted as authoritative.

At the level of language theory CLT has a rich theoretical base. Some of the characteristics of this communicative view of language follow : (1) Language is a system for the expression of meaning. (2) The primary function of language is for interaction and communication. (3) The structure of language reflects its functional and communicative uses. (4) The primary units of language are not merely its grammatical and structural features but categories of functional and communicative meaning.

Discussions of the nature of the syllabus have been central in CLT. Some have argued that the syllabus concept be abolished altogether in its accepted forms. Only learners can be aware of their own needs. Others follow the model proposed by Brumfit which favours a grammatically based syllabus around which notions, functions and communicational activities are grouped.

The range of exercise types and activities compatible with a communicative approach is unlimited. Classroom activities are often designed to focus on completing tasks that are mediated through language or involve negotiation of information and information sharing. Littlewood distinguishes between 'functional communication activities' and 'social interaction activities' as major activity types in CLT. Functional Communication activities include such tasks as learners comparing sets of pictures and noting similarities and differences, working out a likely sequence of events in a set of pictures, discovering missing features in a map or picture etc. Social interaction activities include conversation and discussion sessions, dialogues and role plays, simulations, skits, improvisations and debates.

The role of learner as negotiator between the self, the learning process and the object of learning emerges from and interacts with the role of joint negotiator within the group and within the classroom procedures and activities which the group undertakes. The learner should contribute as much as he gains, and thereby learn in an interdependent way.

Several roles are assigned for teachers in CLT. The teacher should facilitate the communication process between all participants in the classroom and between these participants and the various activities and texts. The teacher should act as an independent participant within the teaching-learning group. He acts as counsellor and group process manager. He assumes a responsibility for determining and responding to learner's language needs. There are numerous textbooks designed to direct CLT. A variety of games, role-plays, simulations and task-based communication activities have been prepared to support CLT classes.

Description of typical classroom procedure used in a lesson based on CLT principles is not feasible. CLT procedures are evolutionary rather than revolutionary.

Total Physical Response

Total Physical Response (TPR) is a language teaching method built around the coordination of speech and action. It attempts to teach language through physical activity. It is developed by James Asher, a professor of psychology as San Jose State University, California. It draws on several traditions including development psychology learning theory and humanistic pedagogy. TPR is linked to the 'trace theory' of memory in psychology. It holds that the more often or the more intensively a memory connection is traced, the stronger the memory association will be. Asher claims that speech directed to young children consists primarily of commands which children respond to physically. He believes that learners can acquire a detailed cognitive map as well as the grammatical structure of a language.

Asher sees first and second language learning as parallel processes. He sees three processes as central. (1) Children develop listening competence before the ability to speak. At the early stages of first language acquisition they can understand complex sentences that they cannot spontaneously produce or imitate. During this period the learner may be making a mental blueprint of the language that will make it possible to produce spoken language. (2) Children's ability in listening comprehension is acquired because children are required to respond physically to spoken language in the form of parental commands. (3) Once a foundation in listening comprehension has been established, speech evolves naturally.

The general objectives of TPR are to teach oral proficiency at the beginning level. Comprehension is a means to an end. The ultimate aim is to teach basic speaking skills. Specific instructional objectives are not elaborated.

The type of syllabus Asher uses can be inferred from an analysis of the exercise types employed in TPR classes. This analysis reveals the use of a sentence-based syllabus, with grammatical and lexical criteria being primary in selecting teaching items. TPR requires initial attention to meaning. Grammar is taught inductively. Imperative drills are the major classroom activities. Other class activities include rule plays and slide presentations. Role plays centre on everyday situations such as at the restaurant, supermarket or gas station. Reading and writing activities may also be explored.

Learners in TPR have the primary roles of listener and performer. They listen attentively and respond physically to commands given by the teacher. Learners are required to respond both individually and collectively. They have little influence on the content of learning. Content is determined by the teacher. Learners monitor and evaluate their own progress.

The teacher plays an active part in TPR. The instructor is the director of a stage play in which the learners are the actors. He decides what to teach. He models and presents new materials. He should be well prepared and well organised. Asher recommends detailed lesson plans. Classroom interaction and turn taking is teaching rather than learner directed. The teacher's role is not so much to teach. He has the responsibility of providing the best exposure to language. In giving feedback to learners, the teacher should follow the example of parents giving feedback to their children. At first parents correct very little. But as the children grow older, parents are said to tolerate fewer mistakes in speech. Similarly teachers should refrain from too much correction in the early stages. As time goes on more teacher intervention is expected.

There is generally no basic text in TPR course. Materials and realia play an increasing role in later learning stages. For absolute beginners, the teacher's voice, actions and gestures may be sufficient. Later the teacher may use common classroom objects such as books, pens, furniture etc. As the course develops, the teacher will need to make or collect supporting materials to support teaching points.

TPR is in a sense a revival and extension of Palmer and Palmer's 'English Through Actions'. It has enjoyed some popularity. Asher stressed that TPR should be used in association with other methods and techniques.

The Silent Way

'The Silent Way' is the name of the language teaching method deviced by Caleb Gattergno. It is based on the promise that the teacher should be silent as much as possible in the classroom and the learner should be encouraged to produce as much language as possible. The student is not a bench-bound listener. The Silent Way views language learning as a problem-solving, creative, discovering activity in which the learner is a principal actor. The cuisenaire rods and the colour-coded charts called Fidel Charts provide physical foci for student learning and recall. The Silent Way is related to a set of premises called 'problem-solving' approaches to learning. These premises are succinctly represented in the words of Benjamin Franklin :

> Tell me and I forget
> teach me and I remember
> involve me and I learn

The Silent Way takes a structural approach to the organization of language to be taught. Language is seen as groups of sounds arbitrarily associated with specific meanings and organized into sentences or strings of meaningful units by grammar rules. Language is separated from its social context and taught through artificial situation. The sentence is the basic unit of teaching. Students are presented with the structural patterns of the target language and learn the grammar rules of the language through largely inductive processes.

Gattegno sees vocabulary as a central dimension of language learning and the choice of vocabulary as crucial. He distinguishes between several classes of vocabulary items. The 'semi-luxury vocabulary' consists of expressions common in the daily life of the target language culture. This refers to food, clothing, travel, family life and so on. 'Luxury vocabulary' is used in communicating more specialized ideas such as political or philosophical opinions. The 'functional vocabulary' provides a key to comprehending the 'spirit' of the language.

Gattegno states that the processes of learning a second language are 'radically different' from learning the first language. Successful learning of the language involves commitment of the self. The self consists of two systems — a learning system and a retaining system. The learning system is activated only by way of intelligent awareness. The learner must constantly test his powers to abstract, analyse, synthesize and integrate. Silence is considered the best vehicle for learning. In silence students concentrate on the task to be accomplished. The retaining system allows to remember and recall at will linguistic elements. It makes linguistic communication possible.

Awareness is educable. As one learns in awareness, one's powers of awareness and one's capacity to learn become greater. The Silent Way thus claims to facilitate what psychologists call 'learning to learn'. Silent Way learners acquire 'inner criteria' that allow learners to monitor and self-correct their own production. It is in the activity of self-correction through self-awareness that the Silent Way claims to differ most notably from other ways of language learning.

The Silent Way is not merely a language teaching method. Language learning through the Silent Way is a recovery of innocence, a return to one's full powers and potentials. The general objective is to give beginning level learners oral and aural facility in the basic elements of the target language. Near-native fluency is aimed at. An immediate objective is to provide the learner with a basic practical knowledge of the grammar of the language. In short the Silent Way teaches learners 'how' to learn a language.

The Silent Way adopts a basically structured syllabus. There is no general silent way syllabus. Language items are introduced according to their grammatic complexity, their relationship to what has been taught previously. Vocabulary is selected according to the degree to which it can be manipulated within a given structure.

Gattegno sees language learning as a process of personal growth resulting from growing student awareness and self-challenge. Learners are expected to develop independence, autonomy and responsibility. Learners exert a strong influence over each other's learning. They are expected to interact with each other and suggest alternatives to each other. They have themselves as individuals and the group to rely on. They must learn to work co-operatively rather than competitively. They need to feel comfortable both correcting each other and being corrected by each other. A learner must also be a teacher, a student, part of a support system, a problem solver and a self-evaluator.

Teacher silence is the most demanding aspect of the Silent Way. Teachers are exhorted to resist their long standing commitment to model, remodel, assist and direct desired student responses. The teacher's role is one of neutral observer, neither elated by correct performance nor discouraged by error. Students are expected to see the teacher as a disinterested judge, supportive but emotionally uninvolved. The teacher is facile and creative. Like the complete dramatist, the Silent Way teacher writes the script, sets the mood, models the action, designates the players and is critic for the performance.

The instructional materials consist mainly of a set of coloured rods, colour-coded pronunciation and vocabulary wall charts, a pointed, and reading/writing exercises. They are used to illustrate the relationships between sound and meaning in the target language. They are designed for manipulation by the students as well as by the teacher, independently and co-operatively.

The 'Fidel' charts are devised for a number of languages. They contain symbols in the target language for all of the vowel and consonant sounds of the language. The symbols are colour-coded according to pronunciation. If a language possesses two different symbols for the same sound, they will be coloured alike. Classes often begin by using 'Fidel' charts in the native language. Students learn to pair a sound with its associated colour. The teacher uses the pointer to indicate a sound symbol for the students to produce. The charts are hung on the wall and serve to aid in remembering pronunciation and in building new words by sounding out sequences of symbols as they are pointed to by the teacher or student.

The cuisenaire rods are used to directly link words and structures with their meanings in the target language. They vary in length from one to ten centimeters, and each length has a specific colour. They may be used for naming colours, for size comparison, to represent people, build floor plans and so on. Use of the rods is intended to promote inventiveness, creativity and interest in forming communicative utterances on the part of the students.

Other materials include books and work sheets for practising reading and writing skill, picture books, tapes, videotapes, films and other visual aids. Reading and writing are sometimes taught from the beginning and students are given assignments to do outside the classroom. These materials are of secondary importance.

A Silent Way lesson typically follows a standard format. The first part of the lesson focuses on pronunciation. Depending on student level, the class might work on sounds, phrases, or even sentences designated on the Fidel chart. At the beginning stage the teacher will model the appropriate sound after pointing to a symbol on the chart. Later, the teacher will silently point to individual symbols and combinations of symbols, and monitor student utterances. The teacher may say a word and have a student guess what symbols comprised the word. The pointer is used to indicate stress, phrasing and intonation. After practice with the sounds, sentence patterns, structure and vocabulary are practised.

The actual practices of the Silent Way are much less revolutionary than might be expected. The Silent Way features characteristics of SLT and Audiolingualism.

Community Language Learning

Community Language Learning (CLL) is the name of a method developed by Charles A. Curran and his associates. Curran was a specialist in counselling and a professor of psychology at Loyola University, Chicago. His application of psychological counselling techniques to learning is known as Counselling-Learning. CLL represents the use of counselling-learning theory to teach languages. Within the language teaching tradition CLL is sometimes cited as an example of a 'humanistic approach.' Links can also be made between CLL procedures and those of bilingual education.

Consider the following CLL procedures. A group of learners sit in a circle with the teacher standing outside the circle. A student whispers a messages in L_1. The teacher translated it in L_2. The student repeats the message in the L_2 into a cassette. Students compose further message in L_2 with the teacher's help. Students reflect about their feelings.

CLL techniques also belong to a larger set of foreign language learning practices sometimes described as humanistic techniques. Moskowitz defines humanistic techniques as those that 'blend what the student feels, thinks and knows with what he is learning in the target language.'

Another language teaching tradition with which CLL is linked is a set of practices used in certain kinds of bilingual education programmes and referred to by Mackey as 'language alternation.' In language alternation a message/lesson/class is presented first in the native tongue and then in the second language. In CLL a learner presents a message in L_1 to the knower. The message is translated into L_2 by the Knower. The learner then repeats the message in L_2, addressing it to another learner with whom he or she wishes to communicate.

Curran himself wrote little about his theory of language. His student La Forge has attempted to be more explicit about the theory of language. The foreign language learners' tasks are 'to apprehend the sound system, assign fundamental meanings and to construct a basic grammar of the foreign language.' La Forge also elaborates on the interactional view of language underlying CLL. Language is people, language is person in contact, language is person in response. CLL interactions are of two distinct and fundamental kinds : interaction between learners and interaction between learners and knowers. Learner-exchanges deepen in intimacy as the class becomes a community of learners.

CLL advocates a holistic approach to language learning, since true human learning is both cognitive and affective. This is termed whole-person-learning. Such learning takes place in a communicative situation where teachers and learners are involved in an interaction in which both experience a sense of their wholeness.

Explicit linguistic or communicative objectives are not specified in CLL. The assumption seems to be that through the method the teacher can successfully transfer his or her knowledge and proficiency in the target language to the learners.

CLL is most often used in the teaching of oral proficiency. With some modifications it may be used in the teaching of writing. CLL does not use a conventional language syllabus. A CLL syllabus emerges from the interactions between the learner's expressed communicative intentions and the teacher's reformulations of these into suitable language utterances.

CLL combines innovative learning tasks and activities with conventional ones. They include :

1. **Translation.** Learners form a small circle. A learner whispers a message or meaning he or she wants to express; the teacher translates it into the target language; and the learner repeats the teacher's translation.
2. **Group work.** Learners may engage in various group tasks such as group discussions of a topic, preparing a conversation, preparing the summary of a topic for presentation of another group etc.
3. **Recording.** Students record conversations in the target language.
4. **Transcription.** Students transcribe utterances and conversations they have recorded for practice and analysis of linguistic forms.
5. **Analysis.** Students analyse and study transcriptions of target language sentences in order to focus on particular lexical usage.
6. **Reflection and Observation.** Learners reflect and report on their experience of the class.
7. **Listening.** Students listen to a monologue by the teacher.

8. **Free conversation.** Students engage in free conversation with the teacher or with other learners.

In CLL learners become members of a community and learn through interacting with the members of the community. Learning is not viewed as an individual accomplishment but as something that is achieved collaboratively. Learners are expected to learn attentively to the knower, to freely provide meanings they wish to express, to repeat target utterances without hesitation, to support fellow members of the community etc.

CLL compares language learning to the stages of human growth. In Stage I the learner is like an infant, completely dependent on the knower for linguistic content. A new self is generated in the target language. In Stage II the child achieves a measure of independence from the parent. In Stage III the separate-existence stage learners begin to understand others directly in the target language. Stage IV may be considered a kind of adolescence. The learner functions independently. The role of psychological understanding shifts from knower to learner. Stage V is called the independent stage. Learners refine their understanding of register. They become counsellors to less advanced students while profiting from contact with their original knower.

In the early stages of learning the teacher operates in a supportive role, providing target language translations. Later, interactions may be initiated by the students and the teacher monitors learner utterances. As learning progresses students become increasingly capable of accepting criticism. The teacher's role is initially likened to that of a nurturing parent. The student gradually grows in ability.

A textbook is not considered a necessary component. A textbook may impede the growth and interaction. Materials may be developed by the teacher as the course develops. Conversations may also be transcribed and distributed for study and analysis. Learners may work in groups to produce their own materials.

CLL is a unique experience. Description of typical CLL procedure is problematic. CLL is the most responsive of the methods. It places unusual, demands on language teachers. The teacher must operate without conventional materials. He must be culturally sensitive and prepared to redesign the language class. Concerns have been expressed regarding the lack of syllabus which makes objectives unclear and evaluation difficult to accomplish.

The Natural Approach

In 1977 Tracy Terrell, a teacher of Spanish in California, outlined a proposal for a new philosophy of language teaching which he called the Natural Approach. It incorporated the 'naturalistic' principles researchers had identified in studies of second language acquisition. Terrell joined forces with Stephen Krashen, an applied linguist, in elaborating a theoretical rationale for the Natural Approach. Krashen and Terrell's combined statement of the principles and practices of the Natural Approach appeared in their book *The Natural Approach,* published in 1983.

Krashen and Terrell have identified the Natural Approach with what they call 'traditional' approaches to language teaching. There are important differences between the Natural Method and the Natural Approach. The Natural Method is another name for the Direct Method. The Natural Approach, as defined by Krashen and Terrell, is believed to conform to the naturalistic principles found in successful second language acquisition. It places less emphasis on teacher monologues, direct repetition and formal questions and answers. There is an emphasis on exposure.

Krashen and Terrell see communication as the primary function of language. Their approach focuses on teaching communicative abilities. The importance of the vocabulary is stressed. Language is viewed as a vehicle for communicating meanings and messages. We are left with a view of language that consists of lexical items, structures and messages. There is no particular novelty in the Natural Approach except that messages are considered of primary importance.

The Natural Approach is for beginners. It has the expectation that students will be able to function adequately in the target situation. They will understand the speaker of the target language and will be able to convey their requests and ideas. Specific objectives depend on learner needs and the skill and level being taught.

Teacher task focuses on objects in the classroom and on the content of the pictures, as with the Direct Method. When learners are ready to begin talking in the target language, the teacher provides comprehensible language and simple response opportunities. The teacher talks slowly and distinctly, asking questions and eliciting one-word answers. There is a gradual progression from Yes/No questions, through either/or questions to questions that students can answer using words they have heard used by the teacher. Charts, pictures and other realia serve as the focal point for questions. Acquisition activities are emphasized. Pair or group work may be employed, followed by whole-class discussion led by the teacher. Techniques recommended by Krashen and Terrell are often borrowed from other methods.

Learners' roles are seen to change according to their stage of linguistic development. They have four responsibilities in the Natural Approach classroom : provide information about their specific goals; take an active role in ensuring comprehensible input; decide when to start producing speech and when to upgrade it; where learning exercises are to be a part of the programme. Learners are expected to participate in communication activities with other learners.

The Natural Approach teacher has three central roles. First, the teacher is the primary source of comprehensible input in the target language. Classtime is devoted primarily to providing input for acquisition. The teacher is the primary generator of the input. Second, the NA teacher creates a classroom atmosphere that is interesting and friendly. Finally, the teacher must choose and orchestrate a rich mix of classroom activities. The teacher is seen as responsible for collecting materials and designing their use.

The primary goal of instructional materials in the NA is to take classroom activities as meaningful as possible. Materials come from the world of realia rather than from textbooks. The primary aim of the materials is to promote comprehension and communication. Pictures and other visual aids are essential. They supply the context for communication. They facilitate the acquisition of a large vocabulary within the classroom.

Krashen and Terrell provide suggestions for the use of a wide range of activities, all of which are components of SLT, CLT and others. A Natural Approach class may start with TPR commands. At first commands are simple. Then use TPR to teach names of body parts and to introduce numbers and sequence. Use visuals to introduce new vocabulary. Combine use of pictures with TPR. In all activities the teacher maintains a constant flow of comprehensible input. He uses appropriate gestures, context and repetition to ensure the comprehensibility of the input. The NA is evolutionary in its procedure.

Suggestopedia

Suggestopedia is a method developed by the Bulgarian psychiartist-educator Georgi Lozanov. Suggestopedia is a specific set of learning recommendations derived from suggestology. Suggestology is a science concerned with the systematic study of the non-rational and/or non-conscious influences that human beings are constantly responding to. Suggestopedia tries to harness these influences and redirect them so as to optimize learning. The characteristics of suggestopedia are the decoration, furniture and arrangement of the classroom, the use of music, and the authoritative behaviour of the teacher. The method has a mystical air about it.

Lozanov claims that his method works equally well whether or not students spend time on outside study. He promises success through suggestopedia to the academically gifted and ungifted alike. He does not articulate a theory of language. He notes that the suggestopedic course directs the student not to vocabulary memorization, and acquiring habits of speech but to acts of communication. He recommends home study of recordings of whole meaningful texts that are above all interesting. The texts should be light-hearted stories with emotional content. Lozanov's recommendation of such stories seems to be entirely motivational.

Suggestion is at the heart of suggestopedia. Suggestopedic learning is built on a particular type of music and a particular rate of presentation.

Suggestopedia aims to deliver advanced conversational proficiency quickly. It bases its learning claims on student mastery of vocabulary pairs. The main aim of teaching is not memorization but the understanding and creative solution of problems. As learner goals Lozanov cites increased access to understanding and creative solutions of problems.

A suggestopedia course lasts thirty days and consists of ten units of study. Classes are held four hours a day, six days a week. The central focus of each unit is a dialogue consisting of 1,200 words or so, with an accompanying vocabulary list and grammatical commentary. The dialogues are graded by lexis and grammar.

There is a pattern of work within each unit and a pattern of work for the whole course. Unit study is organized around three days : day 1 — half a day, day 2 — full day, day 3 — half a day. On the first day of work on a new unit the teacher discusses the general content of the unit dialogue. The learners then receive the printed dialogue with a native language translation in a parallel column. The teacher answers any questions of interest or concern about the dialogue. The dialogue then is read a second and third time in ways to be discussed subsequently. This is the work for day 1. Days 2 and 3 are spent in primary and secondary elaboration of the text. Primary elaboration consists of imitation, question and answer, reading and so on — of the dialogue, and working with the 150 new vocabulary items presented in the unit. The secondary elaboration involves encouraging students to make new combinations and productions based on the dialogues. A story or essay paralleling the dialogue is also read. The students engage in conversation and take small roles in response to the text read.

The whole course also has a pattern of presentation and performance. On the first day a test is given to check the level of student knowledge and to provide a basis for dividing students into two groups — one of new beginners and one of modified beginners. The teacher then briefs the students on the course and explains the attitude they should take toward it. During the course there are two opportunities for generalization of material. In the middle of the course students are encouraged to practice the target language in a setting where it might be used. The last day is devoted to a performance in which every student participates. The students construct a play built on the material of the course. Rules and parts are planned. Students are expected to speak ex-tempore rather than from memorized lines. Written tests are also given throughout the course. These and the performance are reviewed on the final day of the course.

Students volunteer for a suggestopedic course. They are expected to be committed to the class and its activities. Smoking and drinking are prohibited or discouraged in class and around the school during the course. The mental state of the learner is critical to success. Learners must not try to figure out, manipulate, or study the material presented but must maintain a pseudo-passive state, in which the material rolls over and through them. Groups of learners are ideally socially homogeneous, twelve in number and divided equally between men and women. Learners sit in a circle, which encourages face-to-face exchange and activity participation.

The primary role of the teacher is to create situations in which the learner is most suggestible and then to present linguistic material. Lozanov lists several expected teacher behaviours that contribute to learning. (1) Show absolute confidence in the method, (2) Display fastidious conduct in manners and dress, (3) Organize properly and strictly observe the initial stages of the teaching process, (4) Maintain a solemn attitude towards the session, (5) Give tests and respond tactfully, (6) Maintain a modest enthusiasm. Teachers are expected to be skilled in acting, singing and psychotherapeutic techniques.

The instructional materials consist of direct support materials, primarily text and tape, and indirect support materials including classroom fixtures and music.

In a suggestopedia class all participants sit in a circle in their specially designed chairs. The discussion proceeds like a seminar. There are micro-studies and macro-studies. In micro-studies specific attention is given to grammar, vocabulary, and precise questions and answers. In macro-studies emphasis is on role playing and wide ranging innovative language constructions. Then new material is presented and discussed. The seance or concert session is the one by which suggestopedia is best known. At the beginning of this session all conversation stops for a minute or two, and the teacher listens to the music coming from a tape-recorder. He waits and listens to several passages in order to enter into the mood of the music and then begins to read or recite the new text. His voice is modulated in harmony with the musical phrases. The students follow the text in their textbooks where each lesson is translated into the mother tongue. Between the first and second part of the concert, there are several minutes of solemn, silence. Before the beginning of the second part of the concert, there are again several minutes of silence and some phrases of music are heard again before the teacher begins to read the text. Now the students close their textbooks and listen to the teacher's reading. At the end, the students silently leave the room. They are not told to do any homework on the lesson, except for reading it once before going to bed and again before getting up in the morning.

Sugestopedia has probably received both the most enthusiastic and the most critical response of any of the so called new methods.

6

Teaching of English

Teaching of Literature

Literature could be said to be a sort of disciplined technique for arousing certain emotions. One of the main aims in the classroom should be to teach the students to read literature using the appropriate literary strategies. Literary texts have a powerful function in raising moral and ethical concerns in the classroom. The tasks and activities devised to exploit literature should encourage the students to explore the concerns and connect them with the struggle for better society. Literature provides wonderful source material for eliciting strong emotional responses from the students. Using literature in the classroom is a fruitful way of involving the learner as a whole person. Literature involves a special, unusual use of language. It is motivating. It is authentic material. It has general educational value. It helps the learners to understand another culture. It is a stimulus for language acquisition. It spurs students' interpretative abilities. It widens their linguistic awareness. It is highly valued.

English literature teaching is a serious subject of discussion in India. It is claimed that training in critical sensibility and scholarly analysis, fostering of moral and aesthetic values and a sense of national identity and national pride can best be given by teaching our own literature. There is a strong argument in favour of retaining English literature in our curriculum as vehicle for cognitive or cultural content. Unfortunately literature has never been taught in India for providing training in critical sensibility and scholarly analysis. Of the most discussed aspects of teaching — giving information, imparting skills, changing attitudes — literature teaching has remained confined to only giving information. This transmission mode of teaching literature is not limited to India or other non-native countries but in the UK as well. Widdowson wrote : "The usual procedure is to instruct students in a sort of simplified version of literary criticism so that they may be given access to significant aspects of the work they are studying without having to go through the bother of learning to read it for themselves."

The transmission mode of teaching literature presupposes that students are already in command of high-level reading skills in English language. In this approach the most immediate source of reference and inspiration is not poetry or fiction but the pronouncement of critics. Eminent critics' views on the work are transferred from the teacher or source material to the notebook of the student without giving him competence either in literature or language.

Linguistic or stylistics approach to teaching literature was born out of reaction to the subjectivity and imprecision of literary studies. For the appreciative raptures of the impressionable critic, stylistician purports to substitute precise and rigorous linguistic descriptions and to proceed from those descriptions to interpretations or vice versa so as to claim a measure of objectivity. Stylistics is an attempt to put criticism on a scientific basis.

Literary critics' objection is that linguistics uses literature as data for making sociological, anthropological and political statements and not for aesthetic appreciation of literature. Linguists argue that linguistics is interested not only in language but also in language use. Literary text for it is not data for making linguistic statements but for interpretation and evaluation of the literary work. Language is the medium of the work, though it is the language of the author and not the ordinary language spoken around. Hence a study of his language is a must for a proper interpretation and evaluation of his work. Literary critics also point to a defect in the process of stylistics. There is no constraint on the way in which one moves from description to interpretation of the text. The interpretation is arbitrary.

The task of the teacher in the classroom is to teach his learners 'learning' of literature, how to read and interpret for themselves. Literary writings constitute a special domain of linguistic communication and hence they differ from non-literary writings. The creative writers invent special conventions of literary discourse and also use the language system in itself in ways which are unorthodox. Students need a gradual, patient and systematic training in how to read literature and discover the meaning. What is needed is a training in comparison and contrast in the use of the code and communicative conventions of literary writings and non-literary ones. Language and literature are inter-dependent. We need linguistic competence to read literary writings. We need literature to attain communicative competence. Literature has a very important place in ELT. It provides a very rich and widely appealing source of material for reading. It is the repository of language use. It becomes both product and process in a second or foreign language learning situation. In the Indian context teaching literature will meet the needs of our students in comparative studies and attaining communicative competence.

Teaching of Discourse

Language teachers have paid little attention to the way sentences are used in combination to form stretches of connected discourse. They have tended to take their cue from the grammarian and have concentrated on the teaching of sentences as self-contained units. It is true that these are often presented in 'contexts' and strung together in dialogues and reading passages. Basically the language teaching unit is the sentence as a formal linguistic object. The language teacher's view of what constitutes knowledge of a language is essentially the same as Chomsky's : a knowledge of the syntactic structure of sentences, and of the transformational relations which hold between them. Sentences are seen as paradigmatically rather than syntagmatically related. Such a knowledge provides the basis for actual use of language by the speaker-hearer. The assumption that the language teacher appears to make is that once competence is acquired, performance will take care of itself. This assumption is of very doubtful validity. Students entering higher education with the experience of six or more years of instruction in English at the secondary school have considerable difficulty coping with language in its normal communicative use. Widdowson suggested a new orientation in English language teaching. We need language teaching materials which derive from a description of discourse. We need materials which will affect the transfer from grammatical competence, a knowledge of sentences, to communicative competence, a knowledge of how sentences are used in the performance of communicative acts of different kinds.

Language does not occur in stray words or sentences but in connected discourse. Advances in our understanding of our discourse have come from the sociology of language and the philosophy of language. Labov has pointed out that there are certain rules of discourse which cannot be described without reference to social context. Discourse rules have to do with the sequence of actions which are performed in the issuing of utterances.

There are two ways of looking at language beyond the limit of the sentence. One way sees it as text, a collection of formal objects held together by patterns of equivalences or frequencies or by cohesive devices. The other way sees language as discourse, a use of sentences to perform acts of communication. Text analysis and discourse analysis are different but complementary ways of looking at language in use.

The applied linguist Guy Cook presents an alternative approach to the teaching of discourse. According to him social relationship can be seen in terms of three factors : office, status and role. Office is a relatively permanent position within the social structure to which someone is appointed or qualified. Status is a general term for social importance influenced by facts like age, wealth, education. Role is a temporary interactional stance, involving the performance of certain types of perlocutionary and illocutionary acts. Shared knowledge involves hypotheses about the degree of knowledge we share with people we are communicating with and the degree to which the schemata they are operating correspond to our own. This assessment affects every level of discourse, from the quantity and ordering of information to cohesion, the use of the article and grammatical structure. Discourse type is not an academic abstraction but something we all use everyday in order to orient ourselves towards the communication in which we are involved. Discourse types range from recipes and jokes to reports and essays. Discourse structure is the equivalent of generic structure or interaction sequence, while discourse function is the string of rhetorical functions that make up a 'move' in discourse structure. Conversational mechanisms include the gaining, holding and yielding of turns, the negotiation of meaning and direction, the shifting of topic, the signalling and identification of turn type, the use of voice quality, face and body. Cohesion includes reference, substitution, ellipsis, conjunction and lexical cohesion.

The first component of the model is social relationship with its constituents office, status and role. Only one task is presented here. It involves examining a dialogue from a language teaching textbook to determine whether it has successfully captured some of the effects of social relationship. For the second component, shared knowledge, two tasks are worth mentioning : The first takes a short biographical sketch and expands it with information that learners are likely to share with the teacher, then asks the learners to cut out the unnecessary shared knowledge. The second task takes the same short biographical sketch and changes many of the articles, then asks learners to make any necessary corrections. The third component is discourse type. We should alert students to different discourse types so that they may classify the interaction they are involved in. The fourth component is discourse structure. Here Cook refers to tasks such as recognizing and understanding various parts of a text book or associating discourse parts with their discourse types. The fifth component is discourse function. The sixth is conversational mechanism. The last is cohesion. Here Cook proposes to take a passage and replace reference or ellipsis with the full form.

Teaching of Poetry

Poetry is the blossom and the fragrance of all human knowledge, human thought, human passions, emotions, language. Poetry matters because it is a central example of the use of human beings make of words to explore and understand. Like other forms of writing we value, poetry lends shape and meaning to our experiences and helps us to move with confidence in the world we know and then to step beyond it, to respond to the generation of meaning through significant, memorable and deliberated kinds of language. It is an activity to which we are drawn. In its range and rigour we feel both the presence and the pressure of human experience. Poetry embodies delight in expression, stretched between thought, feeling and form.

Poets work at the frontier of knowledge. They are engaged with the struggle for clarity and meaning. They are the guardians of the accumulated richness of our written and spoken inheritance.

When reading is set apart from writing, or every day speech from literature, pupils do not see literature as part of the universal uses of language. The roots of what we call literature are in every day stories, dramas, rhythms, songs, rhetoric and the flow of language in relationships. Literature is a way of keeping words living and accurate. It is the place of poetry in English teaching to help us to restore to pupils a sense of exuberance and vitality in the acquisition of language and in the power and savour of the words.

Ted Hughes in his important and influential book *Poetry in the Making* described two aspects of poetry. His first claim is that poetry is possessed of a certain wisdom, something special, something that we are curious to learn. His second claim is that the latent talent for self-expression in any child is immeasurable. These recognitions are at the heart of reading and writing poetry in schools. The activities in the classroom need to reflect a desire to promote both, in a collaborative endeavour between the teacher and taught.

The current state of the teaching of poetry in many secondary schools does not show much faith either in the wisdom of poetry or in the powers of self-expression of the pupils. Poetry is often neglected and poorly provided for. Its treatment is inadequate and superficial. Many pupils spend much more time completing language exercises of little value than they do reading, writing or talking about poetry. Some English teachers express great unease about teaching poetry. Most English department documents have little to say about the teaching of poetry. Poetry should be encouraged whenever possible. Teacher's attitudes to poetry are crucial in the importance they attach to it; the enthusiasm with which they read it aloud; the extent to which they read it widely themselves; and the way in which they demonstrate a concerned responsibility for it — in short how they give it rank and status. The message children receive about poetry matters much. The ways in which meaning is established for the reader of poetry in the classroom depend upon the associations and contents of the language of the poem reaching into the reader's mind. Pupils need time to make their own responses, to assimilate and ponder before being plunged into talking and writing about what the poem means. Insight into poetry grows with insight into language.

Aims of Teaching Poetry

Poetry is a powerful form of expression. Prose makes an appeal to the head but poetry to the heart. Poetry is a thing of beauty, beauty of form, beauty of language, beauty of thought, mood or feeling. Poetry is an art. It is included in the school curriculum so as to develop the aesthetic sense, the feeling for beauty in the pupils. The aim in teaching poetry is to give pleasure and lay the foundation for an adequate appreciation of what is beautiful in life. It eases the ennui caused by the intensive study of subjects. Poetry is beauty and truth. The aims of teaching poetry are to help pupils read simply constructed good verse with ease, to help then recognise more verses and poems that appeal to the heart and imagination. School is the arena where the total personality of the child is built by the teacher. In the Secondary school curriculum, poetry is enjoined with the purpose of ensuring the pupils' participation in appreciating it as naturally as possible.

Children are quite familiar with the appeal of poetry before they reach school. At school, poetry should be easy and enjoyable. It should elicit emotions and feelings of finer form. Poetry should not be a subject to be examined. Pupils should not be forced to memorize poems. Poetry means much to the adolescent. Adolescence brings greater self-consciousness and a stirring of emotions. The teacher's task should be to present the beauty of poetry before the pupils. Poetry can communicate the actual quality of experience with a subtlety and precision unapproachable by any other means. The teacher should shapen and sharpen the perception of the pupils so as to enable them to create the poem in them by means of the poet's own words. A poetry teacher should bear in mind to pick up an apt poem for his pupils, learn by heart, read it aloud with stress, intonation, rhythm, make the pupils read individually and in groups, keep examination apart and make it an experience.

A sense of appreciation of poetry can be created among the students by cocurricular activities. Arranging regular poetry recitation competition, encouraging the pupils to write English poems and to translate into English simple poems from the mother tongue, can develop a love for poetry. Dramatic versions of poems can be enacted by the students. Students may learn better intonation and widen their knowledge of English poetry by attending lectures delivered by scholars. They should be amply rewarded for recitation and eloquence. All such activities will broaden the cultural and literary activities of the students. For all this the poetry teacher should be a man of poetic temperament.

Teaching of Prose

In English language teaching the teaching of prose occupies an important place. In the early years all language items should be practised before reading. Reading implies reading with comprehension. Reading comprehension involves understanding the meaning of content, vocabulary, grammatical structures and concepts. Reading reinforces the vocabulary. Intensive reading aims at providing practice with sentences of a newly introduced pattern. It concentrates on the study of the language. Extensive reading concentrates on the matter. It is reading for information. Both are important in teaching prose. Extensive reading reinforces the vocabulary and structure. In intensive reading there is model reading by the teacher and loud reading by the pupils. The teacher reads following the stress, intonation and rhythm. The pupil notices the pattern and reads aloud. In Indian schools there is excessive concentration on intensive reading. Most of the teachers are not properly trained. Teachers with other basic degrees than English language and literature are prone to teach English in Indian schools. In consequence the standard of English language learning and teaching is deteriorating. Extensive reading is unknown to most of our students. There are no sufficient library facilities in our schools. It is extremely sad to note that reading habit is not cultivated in young learners of English.

In teaching prose intensively the teacher should proceed as follows :

(a) **Introduction or revision.** The learners are to be brought to the line of learning the material. The teacher should provide a suitable precise introduction or revision.

(b) **Model reading by the teacher.** The teacher should take special care in reading, following the stress, intonation and rhythm.

(c) **Word study.** The new vocabulary is introduced, revealing the different aspects.

(d) **Silent reading by the learners.** The teacher should see that the whole class takes part in the process.

(e) **Testing the comprehension.** The teacher asks questions based on the passage and tests whether they have comprehended the idea.

(f) **Model reading by the teacher.** By now the learners are already familiar with the learning material.

(g) **Loud reading by the pupils.** One of the learners is asked to read the material aloud while the class listens.

(h) **Oral or written exercises.** The vocabulary and structures are revised and reinforced.

In teaching a lesson extensively the teacher may give a brief introduction about the learning material. He may explain the words unfamiliar to them. Comprehension questions may be written on the blackboard. A time limit may be set. Then the learners may be asked to read silently. After it they may be asked comprehension questions. In case of wrong responses by a learner, other learners may be asked to correct them.

A useful technique to remember while reading is known as SQ3R formula. S — Survey, Q — question, 3R — Read, Revise and Recite. Surveying is quick reading, searching for key words and getting an overall impression of the material. The second reading is done by bearing in mind the comprehension questions. The answers to these questions form the central idea of the passage. On the last reading the learner has got answers to the questions. Extra reading should be fostered in the learners.

Teaching Vocabulary

Most of the time in teaching English is devoted to the teaching of vocabulary. Yet even our college students do not have an adequate vocabulary to express simple ideas or to understand a simple passage in English. The teacher must have a clear grasp of some of the aspects of vocabulary. They should know the relative importance of structure and vocabulary, the kinds of vocabulary that an individual uses, the nature of word meaning, the implications of learning new vocabulary and various techniques of teaching vocabulary.

For effective communication one has to master both structure and vocabulary. Structural words are part of the structure. They should be treated as an aspect of grammar. In teaching also they would automatically go with the structure being taught.

F.G. French has made a very useful classification of the words of a language in relation to its users. He divides the words into three groups : (a) the small number of words that a person knows intimately and can use effectively; (b) the relatively large number of words that he understands but does-not normally use; (c) the vast number of remaining words in the language that he does not know. French compares the first group to our 'friends,' the second to our 'acquaintances' and the third to a vast number of 'strangers' whom we do not know.

The user of the language knows the first group of words as intimately as he knows his closer friends. These words constitute his active vocabulary. The second group is far larger than the first group and constitutes his 'passive' vocabulary. The larger a person's passive vocabulary the better equipped he is for reading comprehension. A new word may enter a person's active vocabulary while a known word may be forgotten owing to long disuse in the same manner as we acquire new friends and forget some of the old ones.

If a word has to become part of one's active vocabulary one has to master its spelling, pronunciation and usage as well. Usage means convention or custom in language use. For this knowing the meaning is not sufficient. One has also to know what is and what is not acceptable in the language. The usual practice of giving the meaning of a word in pupil's mother tongue is often unsatisfactory. There are few words in a language which have exact translation equivalents in all contexts in another language. Like human beings a word is known by the company it keeps. Consider the meaning of the word 'table' in these phrases : table of contents, tables of law, a table of card players, multiplication table, table talk, round table conference, time table, to be at the table, to lay the table, to turn the table, to table a motion etc. It is obvious that the mother tongue equivalent for 'table' would not fit in into all these phrases. It is not advisable to teach words in isolation. Even when the teacher has to give the meaning of an isolated word, he should use it in an illustrative sentence. Further, only one meaning of the word should be taught at a time, *i.e.*, the meaning in the text being taught. Pupils should be left to learn the other meanings, if any, when they meet them.

The practice of advising pupils to memorise word-lists straight from the dictionary to increase their vocabulary is useless and ridiculous. In order to learn a word one has to meet it in a variety of contexts. Pupils may be encouraged to make their own list of words they have learnt. This will help them to recall a word when needed.

Techniques of Teaching Vocabulary

The first step in teaching vocabulary is to determine the nature and the relative difficulty of the word. There are many English words which have already entered the pupil's mother tongue *e.g.*, father, mother, sun, moon, cat, dog, eat etc. There are many other words in English which have neither entered the pupil's mother-tongue nor have they exact translation equivalents. The following are some suggestions to teach them :

1. **Actual objects or models.** Names of many things can be taught by showing the actual objects or their models. Nowadays many inexpensive plastic models are available in the market.
2. **Actions.** The meanings of many words can be made clear by performing simple actions in the classroom.
3. **Pictures.** The actions which can be performed in the classroom and the objects and models which can be brought into it are limited. But not so are pictures. Almost any word can be taught with the help of pictures. Every good dictionary makes use of them.

4. **Black board sketches.** Like pictures, a quick black board sketch may work wonders in teaching meaning. Often a mere circle or even a line is sufficient. For example, the basic meanings of some of the prepositions can be taught with simple sketches like the following :

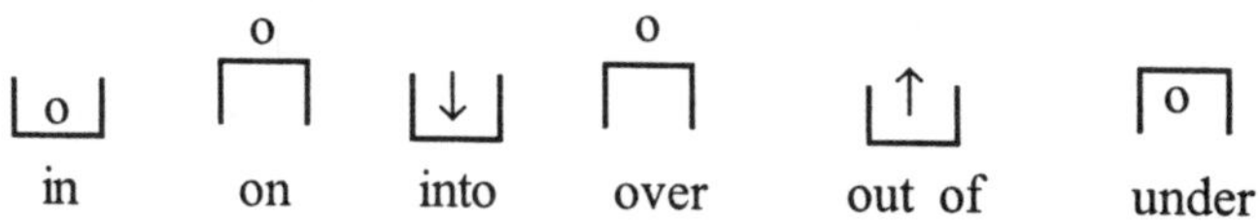

5. **Verbal contents.** There are many abstract words the meaning of which cannot be presented by usual meanings *e.g.,* prefer

   I like coffee more than tea

   I prefer coffee to tea

6. **Illustrative sentences.** An illustrative sentence is very helpful for showing the usage of a word. Every good dictionary makes use of such sentences. The teacher should come prepared with such sentences and use them after pupils have grasped the general meaning.
7. **Synonyms.** If there is an acceptable synonym already known to the pupils, it can be used in sentences to teach the meaning of the new word.
8. **Antonyms.** Like the synonyms, an antonym can also be used.
9. **Word series.** The meaning of a word which forms part of a familiar series, such as the months of the year, the days of the week, the numbers. Similarly there are pairs or series of words which are distinguished by their having favourable or unfavourable connotation.
10. **Associated vocabulary.** It is often easy to teach a number of words together if they relate to a particular topic. For example, it is far easier to teach words like doctor, nurse, patient, medicine, ambulance, stretcher etc. together in the context of 'hospital' than to teach any one of these words in isolation.

11. **Word analysis.** It is sometimes possible to make the meaning clear by breaking up a complex word into its constituent morphemes.

    e.g. : unhealthy ⟶ un+healthy

12. **Definition.** The familiar practice of giving the definition of a word may also be found useful in some cases. In giving such definitions the teacher should be careful to see to it that the definition does not become more difficult than the word itself.

13. **Translation and explanation.** These two become the top favourites with our teachers. But they are the least satisfactory means of teaching vocabulary. Translation and explanation in the pupil's mother-tongue should be attempted when the other means are inadequate or unnecessarily time consuming.

14. **A combined technique.** Quite often no single technique wold suffice. In most cases the teacher will have to use several of them to teach the same item.

The best method of expanding pupils' vocabulary is through extensive reading. Still, some measures can be taken. Pupils may device word families from a basic word by analogy. *e.g.* :

Care — careful, carefully, carelessly, carelessness

fear —

shame —

hope —

joy —

pity —

It may not always be easy to find families of words that are useful for pupils. They can derive useful words by adding familiar affixes.

e.g. : quick — quickly
slow — slowly
move — movement

Word-building games can also be used.

Teaching of Pronunciation

Pronunciation teaching is one of the most important aspects of English language teaching. Every teacher who teaches English by word of mouth is bound to pronounce it and to teach its pronunciation to his pupils. The attitude adopted by the teacher towards the matter of pronunciation has its lasting impact on his pupils. Naturally every teacher must adopt an attitude towards the question of pronunciation. The teacher's attitude may not necessarily be positive; it may even be negative, allowing the students' pronunciation to take care of itself. The only circumstances where the question of pronunciation can be ignored is the teaching of English through distance education.

Pronunciation teaching deals with two inter-related skills — recognition or understanding the flow of speech, and production or fluency in the spoken language. These skills rely very little on intellectual mastery of any pronunciation rules. Ultimately it is only practice in listening and speaking which will give the learner the skill he requires. Debates about innate abilities, linguistic creativity or the pros and cons of habit formation teaching, are hardly relevant to pronunciation.

Pronunciation is the sector of language where the organization of syntax and semantics is converted into motor activity which in turn produce audible sounds. The immensely delicate link between brain and muscles sets pronunciation apart from all other facets of language except writing. It is true that the learning of pronunciation depends more on the students' own ability, mood, age and situation than on teaching. Pronunciation should be taught and taught with more care and expertise than other aspects of language.

The difficulties in learning to produce the sounds of English are mainly associated with the contrasts between the sound systems of the mother tongue and those of English. The teacher should take note of segmental and suprasegmental features which are liable to cause trouble. It is often found that Indians have trouble producing a particular English sound because our languages do not have that sound. No Indian language, for instance, has the exact equivalent of the first sounds of *thin* and *this.* Another factor which causes difficulty to the Indian students of English is the distribution of

English phonemes. A glance at the distribution of English /s/ and /h/ phonemes may make this point clear. The phoneme /s/ occurs in the initial and ultimate positions of words, as in *such, some, sun, sit* and *miss, kiss, less, pass, mass* etc. It also occurs in consonant clusters in both of these positions as in *sky, ship, straw, slight, spring, smash, snake* and *gasp, mist, alms, sense, aesthetics, physics.* The distribution of /h/ is comparatively more limited than that of /s/, for /h/ never ends in English word, or occurs in combination with any other consonant in the same word.

It is very difficult to build up a graded teaching sequence for pronunciation teaching. Even at beginner level all the sounds of English tend to occur within the first few months of teaching. The drilling of isolated sounds is of little value. The teaching sequence must be organised in terms of priorities and degrees of difficulty. The amount of time devoted to specifically pronunciation teaching depends on the larger priorities of the course in general. A useful guide is the precept 'little and often'. The teacher should be prepared to slip a few minutes' pronunciation drill into a lesson at any point where a significant problem is noticed. The teacher should not simply misuse his theoretical knowledge of phonetics.

Pronunciation practice itself might be very short, or may occasionally occupy several minutes. In either case a few key principles should be followed. Recognition practice should precede production practice. Since production reinforces recognition, there is no need to wait for perfect recognition before asking for production. The sounds to be heard and spoken should be clearly highlighted in short utterances. But this should not be taken to the extreme of tongue-twisters like Peter Piper. Students should be given the opportunity to hear the same things said by more than one voice as the model. The English sounds can be demonstrated in contrast with other English sounds or else in contrast with the sounds from the native language. The target sound contrast should be shown to function meaningfully. Students should realise that it makes an important difference to their intelligibility to use it properly. The heart of any drilling or demonstrating of specific sound features is contrast of one kind or another. The ultimate step is the recognition and use of the sound feature in normal speech.

Majority of our students even after studying English for ten years or so find themselves unable to perform quite simple everyday transactions : *e.g.,* make an arrangement, telephone people, state their identity without frequent breakdowns in communication. They cannot respond adequately or appropriately even to simple and straight forward questions. Their utterances are at best slow and laboured and at worst only partly understood. They feel like prisoners of the language — forced to remain silent when they could make a perfectly valid point and trapped into expressing themselves in ways which do not reflect what they think. They are not able to follow lectures and participate in group discussions. They do not know how to behave in the language, how and when to criticise, to apologise or to make suggestions. The problem is that majority of students have difficulty with stress, intonation and rhythm. Their English has been limited to the closely contextualised and highly predicable language of the classroom. They do not appear to have expressed what they feel or think. When put under pressure, they go on making uneasy mistakes.

In countries outside England where English is spoken by a vast majority of people, they do not go in for R.P. accent. We know of the American, Scottish, Irish, Canadian and Australian accents. In English itself we know of dialects such as Western, Northern, Central etc. which are as popular as the RP itself. The typical Indian pronunciation of English suffers in intelligibility. We in India have had a long debate over the issue of a target model of spoken English for teaching purposes. It is high time that we stop making unnecessary fuss of the question of the selection of a model. Let educated Indian English be our model and let us try to describe and document it and subsequently standardize it so that it may be acceptable and intelligible to people in both India and abroad. This variety of English is free from provincialism or the gravitational pull of the mother tongue.

By way of summing up it may be said that the pronunciation teacher may make use of word-association drills, appropriate response drills, question-and-answer drills, contradiction drills, deduction drills etc. These drills are sure to yield expected results and make the teaching of pronunciation lively and exciting. Pronunciation is not to be regarded as a separate area of language learning but as a number of contributory strands in the fabric of English, strands to which teachers and pupils give their attention from time to time.

Aural-Oral Skills

Language is primarily speech. Knowing a language is often defined as the ability to understand and speak the language. Development of the aural-oral skills has a crucial role to play in a second language teaching programme. The two skills are often referred to as 'listening' and 'speaking.' But these terms are rather vague. They do not tell much about the nature of the skills. These complex skills are to be defined in more precise terms. The teacher should know exactly what each of these skills consists of. Equipped with such a knowledge of the component of the skills the teacher can proceed to teach and test them with a greater degree of objectivity.

Various attempts have been made to analyse these complex skills to arrive at their basic components. A person who understands spoken English can :

(a) recognise the characteristic English speech sounds in isolation as well as in combination;

(b) distinguish such sounds from similar sounds in his mother-tongue;

(c) understand the lexical meaning of words in context and grammatical meaning of structures;

(d) understand the meaning conveyed by stress and intonation patterns;

(e) grasp the mood of the speaker and the theme of the discourse;

(f) anticipate words and structures from the context for understanding speech at moral conventional speed;

(g) guess the meaning of an unfamiliar word from the context.

A person who speaks English can :

(a) produce the characteristic English speech sounds and sound patterns, both in isolation and combination;

(b) use appropriate stress and intonation pattens;

(c) use appropriate words and structures to express the intended meaning;

(d) recall words and structures quickly;

(e) organise his thoughts and ideas in logical manner;

(f) adjust his speech according to his audience, situation and subject matter.

The two skills of listening and speaking are grouped together under a single heading 'aural-oral skills' because they usually function together and constitute the basic language skills. The ultimate constituents of a language are its sounds or its phonic substance. Therefore the first requisite for speaking and understanding a language is the ability to discriminate between the contrasting units of sounds in the language. There may be a number of English sounds that are not used in the mother-tongue of the pupils. For example, RP requires two high-front vowels, one long and one short, as in *bead* and *bid* respectively. The first step in developing the aural-oral skills is training the learner to listen for the characteristic English speech sounds including stress and intonation patterns.

Pupils should be trained in listening to connected speech at normal conversational speed. For such listening practice different records and cassettes are available in the market. Passages recorded from the radio can also be used. The teacher himself can speak the passage at normal conversational speed with proper stress, intonation and rhythm.

Passages for listening can be used for either intensive or extensive listening. In intensive listening pupils are trained in detailed comprehension of meaning and identification of particular features of grammar, vocabulary and pronunciation. In extensive training they are trained in gathering information or enjoying stories, plays, poems, etc. Passages for this type of listening can be fairly long. Pupils may be encouraged to listen to radio programmes and see English films and narrate in the class they have heard or seen.

Though listening and speaking go together, it is speaking that makes the learner more active in the learning process. It is necessary to provide maximum opportunity to the pupils to speak the language. Pattern practice can play a vital role in the development of aural-oral skills. There should be sufficient repetition and variety to facilitate habit formation without creating boredom in the class. Pupils should speak the language in meaningful situations. Correction should be selective and based on drilling in the correct form. Persistent crucial errors may be dealt with in a separate remedial lesson.

Reading

Reading is a complex skill involving a number of simultaneous operations. We know very little about the complex mental processes associated with the learning and the use of language. An attempt at an analysis of the skill of reading is bound to be largely speculative in nature.

Silent reading is the more efficient way of reading and more useful in life. Silent reading means reading completely silently, without even moving the lips. The importance of silent reading does not reduce the importance of oral reading at the initial stages of language learning. Oral reading is a useful means of mastering the language code. It is motivating for the young learners. It can be used to practise the structures. It is effective for quick testing of reading comprehension and for improving pronunciation.

The process of reading may be broadly divided into three stages. The first stage is the 'recognition stage.' At this stage the learner simply recognizes the graphic counterparts of the phonological items. For instance, he recognizes a spoken word in its written form. Difficulty at this stage will depend upon the difference between the script of the learner's mother tongue and English, and between the spelling conventions of the two languages. The second stage is the 'structuring stage.' The learner sees the syntactic relationships of the items and understands the structural meaning of the syntactic units. The third stage is the 'interpretation stage.' This is the highest level in the process of reading. The learner comprehends the significance of a word, a phrase or a sentence in the overall context of the discourse. For instance, he comprehends the serious and the jocular use of a word, distinguishes between a statement of fact and a statement of opinion. It is this stage at which a person really reads for information or for pleasure.

The three stages of reading have some correspondence with the three levels of language — phonological, syntactic and semantic. Neither in language nor in the process of reading are these three stages rigidly separated. There is always overlapping and simultaneity of operations.

Mechanics of Reading

When we read, our eyes do not move smoothly along the line of print. They move in jumps. We see only when they rest for a fraction of a second between these jumps. The short pauses of the eyes between jumps are called 'fixations.' The length of print covered between two 'fixations' is called the 'eye span.' A good reader has longer eye-spans and can take in longer stretches of the reading matter. A poor reader has shorter spans and consequently revets his eyes on small bits. He may also move his eyes backwards to look at a word he has missed. This process is called 'regression.' Inefficient reading is usually marked by frequent regressions. Efficient reading includes the ability to comprehend the matter read. In short for proper comprehension an optimum speed is necessary.

Methods of Teaching Reading

The various methods of teaching reading may be broadly divided into two groups : the 'atomistic' and the 'holistic.' The methods may be said to lie as different points on a scale with these two as the two extreme ends.

The Alphabetic Methods. This is an age old method dating back to the days of ancient Greece and Rome. In this method the emphasis is on learning the 'names' of the letters of the alphabet in their sequential order. Pupils are made to memorise words as consisting of these named letters. Now-a-days this method is considered out-dated because memorising the names of letters in a particular sequence has very little relevance to the actual process of reading.

The Phonic or Syllabic Method. This is considered to be an improvement on the Alphabet Method. Here the emphasis is on the sounds of letters. In the case of most of the Indian languages where each letter usually stands for a particular sound, this method works well. Even in the case of English, it does help to learn the pronunciation of a new word.

The Whole-word Method. The word is traditionally regarded as the minimum meaningful unit. The whole-word method seeks to take the word as an individual unit. In this method the learner is taught to read each word as a word picture. The popular look-and-say method of teaching reading at the beginning stages is based on this method. In the look-and-say method the learners look at the words flashed before them and say the words as quickly as possible.

The Sentence Method. This has much in common with the whole-word method except that here the minimum teaching unit is the sentence. This is based on the psycho-linguistic principle of taking the sentence as the minimum unit of thought. The sentence method relies heavily on the principle of situational teaching. We do not generally realize how much we depend upon situations or contexts in understanding language. While listening, we do not listen for individual words. We anticipate an entire sentence from the situation. Even if we do not hear a word or two, we do not have much difficulty in understanding the message. In reading also we proceed from guessing whole sentences from the first few words. If the context is clear, the structures and the words are familiar, teaching reading by the sentence method is psychologically sound.

The Story Method. This is an extension of the sentence method. Here the teacher tells the class a little story to create a verbal context and then present sentences connected with the story. Since the context is known, the pupils do not have much difficulty in identifying the sentences. The story method regards the entire story as the unit of thought.

We infer that no single method of teaching reading is suitable for all occasions and for all learners. The teaching has to use a judicious combination of all the above methods.

Intensive and Extensive Reading

Bacon's dictum 'Some books are to be tasted, others to be swallowed and some few to be chewed and digested' provides a valuable guidance about the kind of reading habits to be developed in our pupils. It implies the pupils should have two types of reading : intensive reading and extensive reading.

In intensive reading, the pupils read not only for detailed comprehension of meaning but also for mastering the structures and vocabulary. The learner can practise the language in his spare time even without a teacher. Intensive reading is still regarded as a very potent means of learning a language. Some experts regard it as only practicable means of learning a foreign language like English.

In extensive reading pupils read for information, or simply for the pleasure of reading. In it the primary object is general comprehension, not language study.

How to teach Intensive Reading

At the initial stage the reading should be mainly confined to the reading of words and sentences from flash-cards or blackboard, following the look-and-say method. For silent reading pupils may be asked to make sentences by joining parts of sentences written on different cards. They may also carry out various activities by following simple instructions written on cards. For instance, instructions such as 'open the door,' 'clear the blackboard,' 'show the class your teeth' etc. may be written on cards, and each pupil may draw a card from the pile and carry out the instruction. This kind of reading should follow oral teaching. Even when the Reader is introduced in the first year, all the words and sentences in a lesson should be presented orally before the pupils are asked to read the lesson. This will give them practice in word-recognition without deciphering meaning through structuring and interpretation. Structuring and interpretation should be introduced progressively.

Teaching Extensive Reading

Structural Readers cannot faithfully present the language that people naturally use in real life situations. A rigid structural syllabus is bound to have an artificiality about it. To remedy this effect, extensive reading material is recommended. Through them pupils come into contact with the natural use of language for development of real communicative competence.

Some books popularly called rapid readers or supplementary readers are specifically prescribed for extensive reading. But they should serve only as a guide. The purpose behind these books is to make the pupils read ungraded material on their own. The teacher's primary concern should be to motivate pupils to read as much of such materials as possible. The proper motivation and guidance can be given by providing the essential background information and then telling the pupils some of the interesting things about the text. To ensure that they read it, he should announce in advance that he would ask questions on the text on a particular day. That day he should allow the pupils to read the text silently once again and proceed to ask questions to test comprehension. Pupils should be made to learn the word meanings by consulting the dictionary at home. The items which are beyond their capacity can be quickly dealt with during the questioning.

It is seen that many teachers do not make any distinction between the Intensive Reader and the Supplementary Reader. This results in insufficient practice of the structures and vocabulary of the Intensive Reader. The very purpose of prescribing the Supplementary Reader is defeated.

Teaching the Structural Reader

The teaching points of a structural syllabus are usually presented through a specially written series of structural Readers in a graded manner. Generally in a six-year course such Readers are prescribed for the first four years only. For the last two years no graded Readers are prescribed. The pupils are expected to have mastered the fundamentals of the language in the preceding four years. The purpose of the text book for these two years is to expand the pupil's vocabulary and to acquaint them with the free use of the language.

To teach a prose lesson of the structural Reader the following procedure is recommended.

Step I. The teacher should ascertain what new structures and vocabulary items are being presented in the lesson. These are shown in the Table of Contents or at the head of the lesson. Then the teacher should teach the structure in an oral lesson. He should also try to introduce as many of the new vocabulary items as possible. All these can be done in separate period and without opening the text. This would ensure thorough teaching of the structures and vocabulary.

Step II. Actual teaching of the lesson is taken up. The text book should be divided into manageable passages and the new words in each passage noted. The teacher may give a preliminary idea of the content of the lesson. He should ensure maximum participation of the pupils.

Step III. The teacher reads out the passage with proper articulation, stress and intonation. The pupils try to follow them.

Step IV. Pupils are now asked to read out the passage silently and try to comprehend it thoroughly. They should be encouraged to consult the dictionary for word meaning and usage and point out their difficulties to the teacher.

Step V. Detailed study of the passage is taken up. The teacher gives word meanings, if necessary, and exercises on grammar, vocabulary and comprehension.

Step VI. After detailed study the teacher asks the pupils to read the passage silently for a second time. He checks their comprehension by means of suitable questions on each point in the passage. Any explanation required is given.

Step VII. Pupils work out some more exercises on vocabulary and grammar. These may be done orally in the class and then given as homework.

Step VIII. Some of the pupils may be asked to read the passage aloud.

Writing

Writing is often regarded as the visual representation of speech. But this is true to the extent that speech sounds can be represented by some marks on paper. It is to be stressed that speech and writing are used in different situations. They serve different social functions.

In face-to-face communication by speech, the physical presence of the speaker and the hearer makes it possible to supplement speech with other non-verbal signals such as gestures, intonation, facial expression, the physical situation etc. The speaker also gets sufficient feedback from the hearer to repeat or rehearse a sentence if necessary to make the message clear. Besides, he need not organize all his thoughts in advance and can even make to do with single words or incomplete sentences. These advantages are not available in writing. There are other devices like punctuation marks, paragraphing, use of capital or bold letters, underlining, italicising, using various types of sentence connections like therefore, however, in other words etc. To communicate through writing one has to learn these conventions besides acquiring the ability to write the letter of the alphabet and spell the words. Further, writing does not come under the everyday use of language. Writing is regarded as the most difficult language skill to acquire.

In second language, teaching writing can be used to fix the structures and vocabulary already taught. Since the development of communicative competence in writing is a slow and ardous process, at the initial stages writing should be viewed primarily as a means of fixing the material taught orally.

The process of writing is usually divided into three stages : manipulation, structuring and communication. Manipulation consists in the psycho-motor ability to form the letter of the alphabet. This is the most rudimentary stage in writing. For second language learners it should not pose much of a problem. In structuring the learner is required to organize the letters into words, and the words into phrases and sentences. This will be easy if writing is preceded by intensive oral work. Communication in writing is the ultimate goal.

Writing usually goes by the name of composition. 'Composition' broadly means 'putting or arranging things in a certain order.' In this sense composition can be started from the very first year of teaching. Of course, in the first year most of the writing exercises will be confined to transcription or copying from the black board. Even so suitable exercises may be devised for pupils to compose.

Guided Composition

Pupils' composition is usually divided into two types : Guided or Controlled Composition and Free Composition. In Guided Composition pupils are supplied with all the necessary structures and vocabulary together with the thoughts and ideas to be expressed. The teacher guides the pupils as to what to write and how to write. As they develop mastery in the use of language this guidance is progressively reduced and finally they are required to write on their own. At this stage they are free to choose their structures and vocabulary and express their own thoughts and ideas on a given topic. This type of composition is called Free Composition.

At the school stage most of the composition should be of the guided type. A new language item should be practised in the order of the skills listening, speaking, reading and writing. So written composition should be preceded by oral composition and practice. In fact Guided composition should be an exercise in putting down on paper, what has been practised orally. In such composition pupils should be required to use only those structures and vocabulary which they have already learnt in their speaking and reading lessons.

The first task in teaching composition is the selection of a suitable topic and finding out the structures and vocabulary required to write the composition. The selection needs thought-free consideration and genuine interest on the part of the teacher. The topic should be interesting and within the experience of the pupils. It should be meaningful for the pupils. Writing letters to friends describing or narrating some interesting things or incidents can be one such meaningful and inspiring activity. Pupils expect the teacher to read their writing. A teacher who goes over their writing, corrects their mistakes and takes an interest in what they have written can still be a ready source of inspiration to the pupils for meaningful writing.

Composition should be experience-based. The pupils should have experience of the subject matter. It should be familiar to them. The structures and vocabulary required for writing should be known to them.

Having decided upon the topic, the teacher should first write out the passage himself in order to find out the structure and vocabulary required. He should then scrutinise his own writing thoroughly. He should know what to teach and how to teach. He should motivate the class to write the passage. He may initiate a brief discussion to introduce the essential new words and structures. The pupils may speak the actual sentences to be used in composition. The teacher should come prepared with a set of well-formulated questions to elicit the sentences from pupils. The pupils should be made to repeat each sentence a number of times. The teacher should write on the blackboard any words that are likely to be mis-spelt by the pupils. If properly done, the oral preparation will greatly reduce errors. The actual writing of the passage can be done in various ways. One is by asking the pupils to write down the questions and then write the passage as answers to these questions. Another technique is to write the passage on the blackboard with some of the words omitted. The pupils supply the missing words as they copy out the passage. Another device is to present the orally drilled sentence in the form of substitution tables. Different elements of the sentences can be put in different columns of the table and the pupils asked to select the appropriate items.

Free Composition

There is little scope for completely free composition in English at the school stage. Such composition presupposes a mastery of the structures and vocabulary required for writing the composition. It is concerned with the logical argument of one's thoughts and ideas on the subject. As such the L_1 seems to be the best medium for practising this skill. Most of the writing of our college students shows that they cannot even put their ideas coherently. The teacher of the L_1 is equally to blame for this sorry state of affairs.

In the upper classes in school when the pupils have acquired a certain mastery in the use of English, they may be allowed to write somewhat freely. Even here some guidance will be required in the selection and organization of the facts and ideas. Having selected a suitable topic the teacher should begin the lesson by imitating a discussion on it. During the discussion he should supply the required facts or direct the pupils to collect them from some specified sources.

The question-answer technique used in Guided composition can also be followed to guide the pupils' thoughts and practise some of the sentences. As the discussion proceeds the teacher should note the points on the blackboard in proper sequence. At the end of the discussion the pupils should be directed to note down the points and develop them into paragraphs.

Paragraph is the basic unit in any connected piece of writing. The pupils' attention should be drawn to the structures of the paragraph. One of the most fruitful exercises for developing the skill of paragraph writing is the study and imitation of model paragraphs. The teacher should select some well-knit paragraphs written in simple English by good writers and help the pupils to study them closely. Ultimately the pupils should try to write a parallel paragraph on a different topic. The teacher himself should have proficiency in this type of critical study.

Letter Writing

One of the common exercises in our schools is letter writing. It can be made highly motivating. It has an immediate audience in view. The exercise is usually confined to memorising a few stereotyped 'letters'.

A letter is essentially a personal communication. It is necessary to take a middle course between the two extremes of memorising stereotyped letters and writing purely personal ones. The teacher should first teach the class the various formal aspects of the letter — the beginning, the body, the closing. He should, then, with the co-operation of the pupils, decide upon a very general theme for a letter. For example, it may be decided to write a letter to a friend, describing a recent event — a cricket match, a picnic, a local festival. Each pupil should then be asked to write to a real friend describing those aspects of the event which he himself considers worth writing about. Or, it may be decided to write a letter to a book-seller, ordering some books. The teacher should supply the names of real booksellers and the pupils should be free to choose the bookseller as well as the title of the books they would like to have. Another interesting device is to have the pupils write the reply to an imaginary letter.

Maximum individual attention is necessary in this type of composition. An energetic and resourceful teacher can keep it within manageable limits by devising a suitable strategy. For example, he may ask the pupils to think of the first sentence each of them would like to begin his letter with. He may then ask some of the pupils at random to say their sentences. He can now correct them, if necessary, and direct them to write it down. He can follow the same technique with each of the subsequent sentences.

The most natural and most motivating situation for writing letters in English is writing to pen friends in foreign countries. It may be too expensive a hobby for our pupils. Pupils may be encouraged to write to pen friends in India.

Dictation

The usefulness of dictation as an aid to learning English is not generally realized. At best, dictating is viewed as a tool to test spelling. But this is a wasteful procedure. There is no point in dictating an entire passage just to test the spelling of a couple of difficult words that might occur in it.

When properly used, dictation can improve pupils' command of the language in a number of ways. For example, it can give effective ear-training for comprehending speech, and linking sound with spelling. It can give practice in the correct use of punctuation marks. It can be an effective device for fixing in the minds of pupils of grammatical structures and spellings of words already taught. It can be a good practice in the manipulative aspect of writing.

A dictation lesson calls for careful advance preparation. Since it is a writing exercise, it should follow speaking and reading. That is, all the words and structures in the dictation piece should be known to the pupils from their speaking and reading lessons. The teacher should tell the pupils a few days in advance what piece will be dictated. He should ask them to come prepared for the task. Even before the actual dictation, he should draw their attention to the spellings of troublesome words, test them orally, and write some of the words on the blackboard. Some of these words may even be kept on the blackboard during the dictation, because dictation is not a test in spelling, and the primary aim is to avoid spelling mistakes.

The teacher should dictate the piece at a reasonable speed. He should take care to say the words in syntactic groups and to use correct intonation and pauses. Pupils should be trained to retain groups of words in their minds while writing. After dictation they may exchange their note books with one another and correct the mistakes under the guidance of the teacher.

The Mechanics of Writing

The first step in writing is the development of the manipulative skill of forming the letters of the alphabet. In teaching English in our schools the pupils will have already acquired some amount of muscle control for writing while learning to write in their mother tongue. It is not necessary to begin by teaching them to make the various strokes, draw circles, squares etc. as is usually recommended for infant schools. They can begin by learning to write the letters straight away. Intensive practice will be necessary. The practice should be systematic. It should be based on a proper understanding of the problems involved. As intelligibility distinguishes good pronunciation from bad pronunciation so does legibility distinguish good handwriting from bad handwriting. In writing legibility depends on maintaining the crucial contrasts between the letters called graphic contrasts. To teach the pupils to maintain these contrasts in their writing, the teacher should first draw their attention to the distinguishing features in apparently similar letters. For example, they should be able to see what makes an *O* different from an *e,* a *p* from a *q*, an *h* from an *n* and so on. This is best done when similar letters are presented in groups. For example, the letters a, o, e, c, d, p, q, g can be presented in one group, m, n, h, r, f, i, l, t, y, u, s in another group and w, v, x, z, k in still another group. Pupils should practise these letters in groups.

From the very beginning the teacher should guide the pupils to make the strokes in the proper direction. He should show where to begin a letter, how to move and where to end. This is really the crucial aspect for developing good handwriting. Strokes in the proper direction will minimise the necessity of lifting the pen and will facilitate joining of letters naturally.

In writing legibility and speed are much more important than the beauty of forms. A person's handwriting like his appearance is unique. No two persons have exactly the same handwriting. Handwriting is traditionally regarded as reflecting the writer's character. Graceful handwriting has great social value and exerts a powerful discipling influence on the mind of the writer. The factors that make handwriting graceful to look at are uniformity of the size of the individual letters, uniformity of the space between the letters, words and lines, and uniformity of the direction and the angle of the slant of the letters.

Teaching Spelling

Pupils make spelling mistakes mainly due to faulty pronunciation, insufficient practice in writing, insufficient visual presentation of words, a general indifference to correct spelling on the part of the teacher and ignorance of the correct rules of spelling. To improve pupil's correct spelling, the teacher should have some idea of the process of acquiring correct spelling. Spelling is more a matter of reflex action than of conscious knowledge. The repeated experiences of writing a word are stored in the muscles of our fingers. When the occasion for writing the word arises, the fingers, as it were, 'remember' the previous experiences and perform the required movements without our conscious effort. The experience thus stored is called kinaesthetic memory and it plays a vital role in all reflex actions. The other sensory aspects are visual memory and auditory memory. To have an active visual memory for spelling, the pupils need repeated and prolonged exposure to words.

The following devices will be found useful for fixing the spelling of troublesome words :

1. Copying. This is the time-honoured device for learning spelling. It is based on the kinaesthetic memory through repeated transcription of a word, to strengthen this memory pupils should practise writing the words without any conscious attention to the task.

2. Delayed Copying. In this technique words on flash cards are shown to the pupils for a very short time. Pupils look at the spelling and write out the word as soon as the card is withdrawn.

3. Dictation.

4. Focusing the trouble spots. Usually it is only a part of the word that gives trouble. The teacher should therefore highlight this "trouble spot" by underlining it or writing the troublesome letters in capitals or with coloured chalk on the blackboard.

5. Use of Mnemonics. Mnemonics are devices which help us to remember something. Pupils can remember difficult spellings by memorising short and simple formulas or sentences that highlight the troublesome part of a word. Pupils can themselves construct their own formulas or sentences to meet their individual requirements.

6. Rules. English spelling cannot be easily reduced to simple rules. But there are a few which are fairly consistent and useful. Familiarity with them will help pupils to avoid some common mistakes :

7. Spelling games. There are numerous language games that can improve pupils' spelling. All of them may not be convenient in the usual class teaching conditions. The following games may be useful.

(a) A few "problem words" are written on a card which is shown to the pupils for a short time. The card is then withdrawn and pupils write from memory as many of the words as possible. The card is again shown and they check the spellings of the words they have written and correct them, if necessary. The pupil who writes the highest number of words correctly wins. Such cards containing the difficult words in each lesson can be preserved and used year after year as a visual aid for teaching the lesson.

(b) The class is divided into two or three "teams." The teacher writes on the blackboard two or three identical columns of words, the number of words in each column being equal to the number of pupils in each team. Each word in the columns has one or two letters missing, usually at the trouble spot. To save time the words can be written before hand on the other side of the blackboard and kept ready for the game. When the teacher gives the word 'Go' pupils from the team come to the board one by one and each pupil completes one word in the column assigned to his team. The first team to complete all the words in the column is the winner.

(c) The teacher writes a long word on the blackboard and the pupils write as many words as they can using only the letters in that word. The pupils using the largest number of correct words is the winner. Alternatively the teacher may write a prefix or a suffix for the pupils to make words with. One special virtue of this game is that it needs no advance preparation.

Grammar

It is very difficult to define the term 'grammar.' Everybody intuitively knows what grammar is. The moment a person distinguishes between a sentence and a non-sentence, he is displaying his knowledge of grammar of the language. Grammar is an attempt to discover patterns in language, structure, an attempt to classify words and sentences and then to deduce certain 'rules.' Grammar, being a scientific study, is descriptive, not prescriptive.

Grammar is said to operate between phonology and semantics. It studies the way in which words/morphemes join to form meaningful sentences. A study of grammar includes the study of five fundamental units of grammatical structure — morpheme, word, phrase, clause and sentence.

The linguistic study of grammar is conventionally divided into two parts — morphology (the study of word structure) and syntax (the study of sentence structure).

The tradition of studying grammar is venerable. The ancient Greeks and Romans, and the medieval Chinese, Arabs and Jews all did important grammatical work on their favourite languages. The rise of linguistics in the early twentieth century gave new impetus to the study of grammar. By the 1930s and 1940s the American Leonald Bloomfield and his successors were doing important work in morphology. In the 1950s Noam Chomsky made the study of syntax one of the most prominent of all areas of linguistics by introducing the new approach called "generative grammar."

Approaches to the study of grammar are many and various. Pre-twentieth century approaches represent "traditional grammar" while most twentieth century grammar are varieties of structuralism. The more formal approaches developed since the 1950s, are known as "themes of grammar." Among the more prominent ones are the several versions of 'phrase structure grammar,' 'lexical functional grammar,' and 'transformational grammar' with its descendent 'Government-and-Binding Theory,' Among the approaches embedded within functionalism, the most prominent is systemic linguistics.

Universal Grammar

Universal grammar refers to the grammatical properties shared by all human languages. When Chomsky introduced his innateness hypothesis in the 1960s, he was arguing that important parts of the structure of human languages are built into our brains at birth. Since about 1980, Chomsky has been elaborating his position and arguing that certain fundamental principles for constructing sentences can be found in all languages and must be part of our genetic endowment present from birth. These principles he collectively terms 'Universal Grammar.'

Naturally, Chomsky attempts to formulate these principles within his own theoretical framework, though that framework has changed dramatically over the years. The principles are abstract.

Traditional Grammar

Traditional Grammar refers to the entire body of grammatical work done in Europe and America before the rise of modern linguistics in the twentieth century. The European grammatical tradition began with the Greeks and was continued by the Romans. The descriptive procedures and terminology they developed eventually came to be applied to modern language like French and English.

The work of the traditional grammarians still form the foundation of modern grammatical work. But we have introduced very many changes and extensions. We reject their insistence on prescriptivism as the basis of description. We recognize many more parts of speech than they did. We assign constituent structure to sentence. We have identified many a large number of grammatical phenomena which they overlooked. We try to construct generative grammars.

Generative Grammar

Generative Grammar refers to a grammar of a particular language which is capable of defining all and only the grammatical sentences of that language. The notion of generative grammar was introduced by Noam Chomsky in the 1950s. It has been deeply influential. Earlier approaches to grammatical description had focused on drawing generalizations about the observed sentences of a language. Chomsky proposed to go further — Once our generalizations are accurate and complete we can turn them into a set of 'rules.' "The 'rules' can be used to build up complete grammatical sentences."

A generative grammar is mechanical and mindless. Once constructed, it requires no further human intervention. The rules of the grammar, if properly constructed, automatically define the entire set of the grammatical sentences of the language. Since the number of possible sentences in any human language is infinite, a successful generative grammar must have the property of recursion : a single rule must be allowed to apply over and over in the construction of a single sentence.

Chomsky himself defined several quite different types of generative grammar, and many other types have more recently been defined by others. A key characteristic of any generative grammar is its power. The larger the number of different kinds of grammatical phenomena the grammar can handle successfully, the more powerful is the grammar. But we do not want our grammars to have limitless power. Instead, we want our grammars to be just powerful enough to handle successfully the things that actually happen in languages.

Within certain limits, all the different kinds of generative grammar can be arranged in a hierarchy, from least powerful to most powerful.

This arrangement is called the Chomsky hierarchy. The goal of Chomsky's research programme is to identify that class of generative grammars which matches the observed properties of human languages most perfectly.

Two of the most important classes of generative grammars so far investigated are 'phrase structure grammar' and 'transformational grammar'. The second is far more powerful than the first. The first is now known to be just slightly too weak.

Transformational Grammar

In the 1950s Noam Chomsky introduced into linguistics the notion of a generative grammar, which has proved to be very influential. Now there are very many different types of generative grammar which can be conceived of; Chomsky himself defined and discussed several quite different types in his early work. But, from the very beginning, he himself favoured a particular type, to which he gave the name "transformational grammar" or T.G. TG has sometimes also been called "transformational generative grammar" or TGG.

Most types of generative grammar in which any body has ever been interested can be usefully viewed as working like this : starting with nothing, the rules of the grammar build up, structure of a sentence piece by piece, adding something at each step, until the sentence structure is complete. Crucially, once something has been added to a sentence structure, it must remain; it cannot be changed, deleted or moved to a different location.

TG is hugely different. In TG the structure of a sentence is first built up in the manner first described, using only 'context-free rules,' which are a simple type of rule widely used in other types of generative grammar. The structure which results is called 'deep structure' of the sentence. But after this, some further rules apply. These rules are different in nature. Transformations have the power to change the structure which is already present in a number of ways. They can add new materials to the structure. They can also change material which is already present in various ways. They can move material to a different location. They can even delete material from the structure altogether. When all the relevant transformations have finished applying, the resulting structure is the surface structure of the sentence.

TG is thus a theory of grammar which holds that a sentence typically has more than one level of structure. TG has developed through a number of versions, each succeeding the other. In his 1957 book *Syntactic Structures* Chomsky provided only a partial sketch of a very simple type of transformational grammar. This proved to be inadequate. In his 1965 book *Aspects of the Theory of Syntax* Chomsky proposed a very different and much more complete version. This version is variously known as the Aspect Model or as the standard theory. All textbooks of TG published before 1980 present the standard theory.

Deep Structure

'*Deep Structure*' is an abstract representation of the structure of a sentence posited by a linguist for analytical purposes. The concept of 'deep structure' was a central part of the first versions of transformational grammar, introduced by Chomsky in the 1950s.

Chomsky's idea was that certain important generalizations about the structure of the sentences in a particular language were difficult to state in terms of the surface structure of the sentence. But these generalizations could be readily expressed in a theoretical framework in which sentences were assumed to have abstract underlying forms.

Chomsky defended his idea by appealing to examples like *John is eager to please* and *John is easy to please.* On the surface these may appear to have identical structures but they receive very different interpretations. Using the symbol NP for a noun phrase, which is in some sense missing on the surface, we might posit deep structures for these two sentences : John is [eager to please NP], but [NP to please John] is easy. These representations now allow us to explain the meaning of each sentence. They must be modified by the action of powerful rules called transformations.

The conception of deep structure has changed substantially over the years. The several successive versions of TG have involved very different views of deep structure. Consequently different textbooks will present significantly different versions of it. Most theories of grammar other than TG have declined to recognize a concept of deep structure.

Surface Structure

Surface structure refers to the syntactic structure which is most obviously assignable to a particular sentence. Every sentence in every language has some kind of syntactic structure. Consider the following English sentence : *Susie is hard to please.* The structure assigned to this sentence may vary. The majority may analyses it as follows : it consists of a subject NP *Susie* and a predicate *VP is hard to please* : the latter in turn consist of a verb *is* and an adjective phrase *hard to please;* the adjective phrase in turn consists of an adjective *hard* and a verb phrase *to please.* We can represent this structure schematically as follows :

[Susie] [[is]] [[hard]] [to please]]]

Now this structure is the surface structure of the sentence. It is the syntactic structure which we would most naturally assign to this sentence.

Government

'Government' refers to the grammatical phenomenon in which the presence of a particular word in a sentence requires a second word which is grammatically linked with it to appear in a particular form. Most English personal pronouns occur in two different case forms — the nominative and the objective, *e.g.*, I/We, She/her, they/them. When a preposition takes one of these pronouns as its objects, that pronoun must appear in its objective forms : *with me,* not *with I, for her,* not *for she.* We say that the proposition governs the case of its objects. It is the very presence of the preposition which requires the objective case. This is not 'agreement.'

Government can be more complex. In German, for example, there are several different cases and some prepositions govern one case, others another.

Verbs can also govern case-forms. In Basque, for example, a particular verb may govern objects in any of several cases.

In the Government-and-Binding Theory, the concept of government is generalized.

Government-and-Binding Theory

Government-and-Binding Theory is a particular theory of grammar, the descendent of 'transformational grammar'. During the 1960s and 1970s Chomsky's TG went through a number of substantial revisions. In 1980 Chomsky gave a series of lectures in Pisa, outlining a dramatic revision of his ideas. These lectures were published in 1981 as a book *Lectures on Government-and-Binding.* The new framework presented there became known as the Government-and-Binding Theory (GB) or as the 'Principles-and-Parameters approach.'

GB represents a great departure from its transformational ancestors. Still, it retains a single transformational rule.

GB is based upon two ideas. First, the grammars of all languages are embedded in a universal grammar, conceived as a set of universal principles applying equally to the grammar of every language. Second, within universal grammar, the grammars of particular languages may differ only in small and specified respects. These possible variations are conceived as parameters.

GB is a modular framework. Its machinery is divided up into about eight distinct modules or components. Each of these modules is responsible for treating different aspects of sentence structure. Each is subject to its own particular principles. A sentence structure is well-formed only if it simultaneously meets the independent requirements of everyone of the modules. Two of those modules — those treating government and binding — give GB its name.

GB sees every sentence as having both an abstract underlying structure (the former deep structure now renamed D-structure) and a superficial structure (the former surface structure now renamed S-structure). There is also a third level of representation, called logical form (LF). Certain requirements apply to each one of these three levels. Further requirements apply to the way in which the three of them are related.

Teaching of Syntactic Structures

The syntactic structure or arrangement of words in larger units — phrases, clauses, sentences — is the most important aspect of language. The grammar of a language is often looked upon as a set of rules governing the syntax of the language. The structural syllabus is a scheme for teaching the grammar of the language. For effective structural teaching the teacher must have a clear grasp of the teaching material. He must also be able to appreciate the roles of conscious knowledge and unconscious habits in acquiring the mastery of the language. Every lesson based on the structural syllabus should be regarded as a lesson in functional grammar, that is the grammar that functions in the correct use of the language. The structure should be taught before teaching the reading lesson. Also the new words to be taught should also be from the reading lesson.

The structural syllabus is based upon the principle of cumulative approach. One structure is sought to be built up on a previously taught lesson. Before introducing the new structure the teacher should ascertain through proper questions that the pupils know the relevant previous structures. This procedure conforms to the psychological principle of proceeding from the known to the unknown. It is motivating the pupils. The item selected as previous knowledge should be relevant.

Proceeding naturally from the previous knowledge, the teacher should introduce the new structure in appropriate situations. He should take care to use in the new structure the words already known to the pupils. He should use it a variety of situations and give suitable illustrative examples. He may ask the pupils say and write down a few of the sentences.

Mastering of language depends on practice. The practice should be based on an intelligent understanding of the grammatical point involved. The extent and depth of this understanding will depend upon the level of maturity and experience of the learner. The pupils should be given some opportunity to study the peculiarities of the structure through a process of comparison and generalisation. The pupils may arrive at a rule with the teacher acting as a guide. They will be able to make the rule if the teacher takes care to supply, an adequate number of examples. Acquiring the grammar of a language is a slow process. The teacher should resist the temptation of teaching too many items in the same period.

When the pupils have had some understanding of the peculiarities of the structure, the teacher should proceed to organise practice. This should be mainly oral, followed by some amount of practice in reading from the black board, flash cards, substitution tables etc. and writing transcription and controlled exercises in sentence construction, sufficient time should be devoted at this stage.

When the pupils have acquired a fair degree of mastery of the structure, the pupils should use it in new situations. This can be done by varying some of the situations used earlier in the lesson. The meaning of the new words should be made clear before they are used by the pupils. This can be done in various ways, depending on the nature of the word. The correct pronunciation should be given. Finally some exercises should be given to practise at home. The exercises should be real practice material, and not test items.

Teaching Formal Grammar

In teaching formal grammar, the principles and procedures suggested for functional grammar lessons may be broadly followed. The comparison and generalisation can be done simply by collecting the examples from the pupils. The teacher has only to devise a suitable technique to collect the examples from the pupils. This can be done with well-planned oral questions. Or a special passage incorporating all the examples may be written out. A lesson in formal grammar may proceed on the following lines : motivation and testing of previous knowledge, collection and presentation of examples, comparison and generalisation, application of the rules.

Audio-Visual Aids

Much of what we say in any language is promoted by what we see or have seen around us. We, therefore, have to give our students practice in reacting in English to objects or pictures. Audio-visual aids are an addition to our "armoury." They allow us to explain a word or concept simply by showing a picture or pointing to an object. Abstractions can often be expressed in this way where mime or words are insufficient. Time can be saved by passing pictures or objects round the class and getting group work going. Tempo can be accelerated because showing or pointing is a more rapid process than speaking or explaining. One should not become intoxicated with visual aids. They can deteriorate into poor substitutes for preparing a lesson. Combine them with other teaching techniques to fulfil immediate and long-term aims. The more the pupil is exposed to good models, and the more relevant the material handled appears to him, the more likely he is to make the considerable effort needed to speak a language well.

In the classroom, the teacher tries to provide a stimulus to many things at once — accuracy of hearing and imitating, understanding of groups of foreign sounds and reaction to the ideas expressed by these sounds. How much of what goes on in the classroom the pupil will retain after leaving the lesson depends on his own interest in the subject and his own linguistic ability and on the teacher's ability to get at the individual member of the class. There can be no question that the physical personality and the linguistic technique of the teacher will always have a far more profound and lasting effect than any mechanical aid.

It has become fashionable to talk of radios, tape-recorders, television and language laboratories as the most important aids in teaching English. This has developed in the teachers of our country a cynical attitude towards all teaching aids. They regard teaching aids as something which only the affluent schools can afford. This is but natural in a country where the vast majority of schools do not have even the minimum essential furniture like desks and benches in their classrooms. All aids need not be as expensive as the radio or the tape recorder. Nor should they sound as unrealistic as the advocacy of closed circuit television or language laboratories for our rural schools. Many of the more useful aids can be made by the teacher himself at little or no cost at all. What is required is a proper understanding of the purposes of the aids and a genuine desire to improve one's teaching.

The Blackboard

The blackboard is one of the most important visual aids, commonly available and inexpensive. It has the advantage of providing a focal point of attention for the whole class. It can be used for a variety of purposes. However, it is very easy to forget its usefulness, simply because it is always there, or to use it ineffectively through lack of thought, preparation, and reluctance to regard it as an integral part of a lesson.

A good blackboard should have ample space. Before writing anything on the blackboard, it is advisable to mentally divide the blackboard space into two parts : a reference area and a working area. Use of coloured chalk will help in focusing pupils' attention and will make the lesson interesting. The writing on the blackboard should be neat and tidy and clearly visible from the last bench. The teacher should be careful not to stand for a long time writing on the board with back to the class while students do nothing. He should not talk to the board. If he needs to say something, turn around and address the class. Keep the students involved by getting them to read and repeat parts of what you have written. The teacher can get the pupils write on the board for him and test their spelling this way. The teacher should clean the board when it becomes impossibly crowded, instead of squeezing in additional sentences wherever, there is space.

The blackboard can be used for developing aural-oral skills. The teacher can write words and sentences to enable the pupils to associate the sounds with their written forms. Model sentences, cue words, questions, substitution tables etc. can be put upon the board for pattern-practice drills. For situational teaching, various situations can be created with the help of simple sketches on the blackboard. Children can imagine a great deal and they readily accept make-believe. Indeed, they would sooner accept a quickly drawn four line sketch, as a 'box' than wait for the teacher to draw a proper figure of a box. Once a sketch has been identified as something real, they keep up the pretence and love it. A little practice in drawing matchstick figures will stand the teacher in good stead. One great advantage of blackboard sketches over pictures is that the pupils can see a situation or a story developing right in front of their eyes.

The blackboard is an ideal aid for developing reading and writing skills. It can be effectively used for making the meaning of words clear. The teacher can put the comprehension questions on the board, and engage pupils to find out the answers from the reading passage. The blackboard can be used to show the beginners how to write the letters of the alphabet. Since the teacher will be writing right in front of them, they will be better able to make the strokes in the proper direction by imitating him. Asking the pupils to write on the board may not always be advisable, because it is time consuming. Where possible, small blackboards can be put up on the side walls at an appropriate height for exclusive use of the pupils. Whenever a new word is introduced it should be written down on the board. For free composition, writing letters, applications, the blackboard is a useful aid. For teaching grammar the blackboard is an unavoidable aid.

Many teachers find it convenient to use a roll-up board. It is a simple device consisting of a piece of dark-coloured sheet with two battens or rollers at top and bottom, fixed in the manner of a wall-map. It is readily available. It can serve most of the purposes of the blackboard. It can be conveniently carried and put up in the classroom. The teacher can write the material leisurely during off time and put it up the right moment in the lesson. This saves time and relieves the teacher of the avoidable burden of carrying the material in his head and writing it properly during teaching.

Charts and Tables

Large wall charts and tables can be used for the development of all the four skills as well as for imparting the essential knowledge of structures and vocabulary. Pupils can read sentences from charts and tables and write them. Large readymade substitution tables may be found very helpful. Many charts and tables on the syntactic structures and vocabulary are available in the market.

In the early years the pupils can read sentences and rhymes from charts. In teaching grammar, the examples for generalization and comparison can be written on charts and used year after year. In such charts colours can be used to focus attention on a particular point. Illustrative sentences on all new words in a lesson can be written on a chart and displayed at the appropriate stage. Suitable model paragraphs can also be written on charts to enable pupils to write parallel paragraphs. Each school should try to have a good collection of such charts and tables. Each item should have 'instructions for use' written on the back.

Flash Cards

Cards containing letters, words, phrases, sentences etc. are a very useful and inexpensive aid in teaching English. The letters in the cards should be sufficiently large so that the whole class can read them without difficulty. These cards can be used for a variety of purposes. For teaching reading by look-and-say method they are indispensable. Pupils can practise sentence-making words-making by combining the parts written on these cards. They can be used in teaching spelling by the technique of "delayed copying." This can be extended to copying of sentences.

Cut-outs

Small figures of people, animals, birds, cut-out from magazines and newspapers can be excellent teaching aids. If they are mounted on cardboard, they would become more versatile and durable. The mounted pictures look almost like three dimensional models. They can be used like puppets to create interesting groups and situations. A collection of cut-outs stored under different labels such as A family group, A Road Accident, In the Market, On the Field etc. will be an invaluable aid for the teacher.

The Flannel Board

When a small piece of cloth with a rough surface is pressed lightly against a cloth with a similar surface, it sticks on the cloth, much in the manner of cotton wool or fluff sticking on woollen cloth. Therefore, if a board is covered with such a sheet of cloth and a piece of such material or sandpaper is pasted on the back of a cut-out, the cut-out will stick on the board when lightly pressed against it. Such a board is called flannel board. The board has a great advantage in that pictures can be arranged and rearranged with the greatest ease. Various actions can be shown by putting up or taking off pictures in quick succession. Instead of having a board covered with flannel, it is also possible to make an improvised flannel board by simply throwing over the blackboard a piece of old blanket or similar cloth. The pictures or cards can also be backed with similar material or pieces of coarse-grained sandpaper. The pupils will be delighted by this aid.

Wall-pictures

Large pictures showing, for example, a street scene, a market place, a playground etc. can be very effective for oral practice and for writing connected sentences. A series of such pictures can be used to narrate a story. Wall pictures are available in the market, but a teacher can easily make his own. The picture need not be perfect. Figures can be traced from magazines or drawing books. Even cut-outs can be pasted on a large sheet of paper to make an interesting wall-picture. Use of a variety of colours will make the picture more attractive.

The Flip-chart

If two cardboard sheets are hinged up at the top, they can be made to stand on the table with the two sheets forming the two sides of a triangle and the surface of the table forming its base. A series of pictures depicting a story or an incident can be pasted on cardboard and hinged together in this manner, and the sequence can be shown to the class by turning over the pictures one after another. Such a device is called a flip chart. It can be carried conveniently. It can be used with great effect to rouse the curiosity of the pupils.

Cue-sheets

Slips of paper containing cue words and sentences can be used very effectively for organising oral practice. Such slips are useful in group work. Pupils in two rows can sit facing each other and, by looking at the cue sheets, put and answer questions. Once this activity is set in motion it can go on without the intervention of the teacher.

Advertisements

Some advertisements can be excellent aids in teaching English. A good advertisement attracts attention to itself and its slogan is striking enough to be remembered easily. By displaying carefully selected advertisement in English and encouraging the pupils to collect such advertisements the teacher can help them to learn many useful patterns embodied in the slogans. Some advertisements deliberately violate grammatical rules or coin new words. They may highlight a syntactic or morphological rule. They can be profitably exploited to fix the rule in the minds of the pupils.

The Gramaphone

In the early stages of learning a new language it is very helpful to reinforce the teacher's personal effort with a short session of listening to and careful imitation of suitable recorded material. Pupils are more ready to accept what the teacher says and does if the record illustrates the same points and thus seems to be an authentic check on what the learners are striving to do. It is amazing how well young children can imitate every inflection, vowel quality and intonation of a record. Perhaps the best feature of a gramaphone record is that a child can have it at home and play it again and again in his own time. This extension of experience is invaluable in spurring on the individual, for undoubtedly children know what they like and like what they know.

The Tape Recorder

A tape recorder is an essential classroom aid. It brings other voices into the classroom. It gives the pupils valuable practice in listening to varieties of English different from the teacher's. A great deal of material is available on tape. The tape recorder has now found its way into the majority of schools. The most obvious use of the tape recorder in the classroom is to give pupils salutary lesson of hearing their own voices. Until we have heard ourselves on a tape, we have little real idea of what our voice sounds like to other people. The first impact on the hearer is one of shock. When the children have got over this initial impact and the fun of hearing each other, the real work can begin. Its best remedial function is with small groups. Do not use it too much too often. Choose the material carefully — say two sentences illustrating certain points of pronunciation or intonation. Practise them with a small number of pupils before recording. Then record their voices straight off. Play the recording back straight through and let the whole group hear the accurate record. The teacher can make criticisms as the lesson proceeds.

The tape recorder can also be used for dictation at all levels. The teaching and learning of poetry is a very rewarding occupation. The best way to learn a short poem is to hear it again and again as a whole. Children only learn to say a poem well if they hear it well read or said. Poetry is something which must be taught, even in one's native language. There are many possible variations in the technique of teaching poetry. There is not one correct and definitive interpretation of a poem. The rhythm must be clearly defined, pauses and stresses carefully marked. In teaching drama the tape recorder can be a valuable ally. Some pupils can be encouraged to listen to foreign broad-casts and record anything which appeals to them.

Overhead Projector

The teacher may write or draw on a transparency and project it on to a screen. The transparencies can easily be added to, while the lesson is in progress. The overhead projector is a very useful alternative to the blackboard in that the teacher does not have to turn his back on the students. The teacher can save time by preparing the material in advance. Another advantage over the blackboard is that the OP does not have to be cleaned and there is more space available. It is used in much the same way as the blackboard — for writing model sentences, presentation, explanation, drills, pictures etc. Some commercially produced transparencies are also available. Overhead projector transparencies can be flexibly used.

Slides and Film Strips

Film strips are similar to slides except that they are easier to use. Both film strips and slides have the same function as all wall charts, flash cards or pictures for oral composition. The advantage is that we can move from one to the other more easily once the equipment is set up. The teacher can make his own slides for any form of lecture. Slides and film strips are particularly useful for any series : for instance, a routine day in someone's life, or talking about places, or for some specialist subjects.

Film

Obviously, film accustoms students to understanding English in the cinema or on television. Usefulness can be increased by making sure of 'feedback'. Choose specialised films for different profession; see the film before it is shown to the pupils so that you can determine level and suitability of content, stop the film from time to time, and get students to ask questions, if they have not understood. Then, ask them questions about events, character, descriptions etc. Give the pupils a script of the film, after they have seen it. Get them to go over it for homework and ask them to write a summary, or to give an oral account the next day. However much you use films in class, also encourage the pupils to go to the cinema and watch television. Films can also be used more directly in class. Video can be used effectively in language teaching. The computer is considered very sophisticated aid in language teaching. But it is very effective. In the coming years they may play key roles in English language teaching in India.

The Language Laboratory

Much of language learning is the learning of complicated skills. Learning skills is largely a question of adequate and effective practice. Basically a language laboratory is a long classroom in which the students are isolated from each other by sound proof walls. These walls prevent the sounds made by anyone student from reaching his neighbours. This leaves him free to practise speaking without disturbing them. A whole class of students can practise speaking at the same time instead of one after another as in the conventional classroom. In this way language laboratories can help to save time. This is a rather simplified description of the functions of the language lab. Language lab is a powerful aid if properly used, a waste of time and money if improperly used. The language lab is a tool, and like any tool, useful only in the hands of a craftsman who knows how to use it.

Language labs may have quite simple equipment in which case the sort of practical work possible is limited; or they can be very lavishly equipped and thus very versatile in their use. The more versatile they are, the more complicated they tend to be for the teacher and the student to operate. Anyone setting a lab should start with the simpler equipment. Experience has shown that the initial installation of the most complicated form of language lab has often been followed by confusion and discouragement on the part of the teacher and loss of interest on the part of the students.

There are three stages in the development of a language lab from the simplest to the most complex. In the first stage it consists of a number of sound proof booths each containing a set of headphones connected to a microphone in front of the teacher. In this set up the student can listen to the teacher and carry out his instructions, copy his speech, answer his questions and so on, all at the same time. The first refinement within this stage is to connect the students to the output of a gramaphone or tape recorder. This leaves the teacher free while the students continue to practise. The weakness of this arrangement is that the teacher cannot check up on the students' work. He does not know whether they are practising correctly, persisting in their mistakes, or indeed practising at all.

In the second stage the teacher has earphones and is connected with a microphone in each student's booth. We now have two-way communication. The teacher and the individual student can speak to each other, and the teacher can listen to and monitor any student's production and advise him how to improve. The student can also speak to the teacher and ask for an explanation or help.

The third stage of development sees the introduction in to each student's booth of a tape recorder. Now the student can record his practice efforts together with those of the model. The teacher is able to monitor the individual works of all his pupils, if he wishes. The tape recorder in the individual booths can now play back pre-recorded practice tapes to the students independently of all the other members of the class are doing or even out of class-time. At this point the last refinement is introduced. Special dual-track tape recorders in the students' booths on which the master's model can be played and the students' copy recorded all in one operation.

The student has now achieved complete independence from the teacher.

To sum up, so far we have three stages of development :

Stage I : (a) The teacher can speak direct to all students together.

(b) The teacher or the recorded material can speak to all students.

Stage II : (a) In addition to facilities available in stage I, individual students can speak to the teacher and the teacher can monitor their practice.

(b) The teacher can now speak to any student individually.

Stage III : (a) In addition to the facilities in Stage I and II students can record the teacher's and their own voices on their single track tape recorders.

(b) Students can play individual tapes on their dual track recorders and simultaneously record their own responses.

The language lab is for practising aural-oral skills. These skills are more especially applied to learning language material in the fields of pronunciation and grammar. Any materials and methods used for practising the oral skills in these fields in the classroom are appropriate and can be adapted to the language lab. Thus procedures such as listening to, identifying, distinguishing between and copying sounds, stresses, tones and tone patterns in pronunciation and ear training are possible. In grammar the familiar drills of substitution, completion, prepared conversation and the like are appropriate. The lab can be used for asking and answering questions, informal oral testing and more formal oral examination. It has its place in the earlier stage of language learning as also in its most advanced stages but never can it replace the teacher or take over the whole teaching burden. It must always be a tool, no master.

The possession of a language lab does nothing to lighten the teacher's task. The preparation of materials for use either 'live' or recorded in the lab increases the teacher's work considerably. The teacher cannot improvise in the lab. He cannot find adhoc practice material in the course of the lesson as he can in the classroom. He cannot rely on intuition. Laboratory work must be more carefully and more fully prepared even than class-work. Nor must the teacher imagine that material prepared for one year can be used unchanged the next. The lab is voracious of the teacher's time and energy.

In the lab-as-an-aid point of view the teacher is clearly thought of as the central figure teaching the students. The lab is one more aid, not the central component of teaching. The lab materials are designed to supplement class work selectively. The materials are not complete lessons. Language labs are not meant to solve the problem of teacher shortage. Language labs require better prepared teachers.

The language laboratory became a controversial issue immediately it was introduced. There were those who attacked it as a mechanical soulless device which would eliminate the teacher. Many saw it a solution to teaching problems. It is expensive to buy and costly to run effectively. Like a car it has to be properly maintained.

Syllabus

The Grammatical Syllabus

The grammatical syllabus is a response to the question 'how do users of the target language express themselves?' Such a syllabus assumes that the learner's need is for items which can cope with a grammatical demand. Most language teaching materials derive from grammatical syllabuses and accept the view that language is a grammatical system. It matters little whether the psychological orientation of the syllabus designer is behaviourist or cognitive.

The grammatical syllabus presents several problems. The "grammar" accepted by the designer is context-free. The unit is the isolated sentence. The assumption is that the essential problem for the learner is to master linguistic form and only secondarily the social meaning and use of such forms. A grammar is at its most efficient when it presents together forms which are subject to the same rule. The assumption that knowledge of the grammatical code equals ability to use that code is quickly seen to be false by the learner. The effect of this may well be to lower his motivation. The aim of teaching the whole of the grammar may be inefficient. It is a virtually unattainable goal. Few learners will ever need the whole of the grammar in order to communicate. In short, a purely grammatical syllabus presents linguistic items to the exclusion of other elements of the language.

The Situational Syllabus

A true situational syllabus — none exists so far — would try to provide the learner with the knowledge and skills he would need to deal with social demands. The question would be when and where will the learner need the target language? Such a syllabus would assume that language consists of patterns of social use. Language learning implies becoming proficient in using the language in social situations. A truly situational syllabus would take the setting of the use of language as primary and the linguistic forms dependent on the situations. Linguistic items would be selected on the likelihood of their occurrence in a particular social context.

The pure situational syllabus would also present problems. It assumes that the syllabus designer is able to predict accurately the situation in which the learner will find himself. It further assumes that the components of the concept situation have been exhaustively listed and their inter relationships mapped. Another assumption is that there is some predictable relationship between the situation on the one hand and the language used in it on the other. Unfortunately there are no strong relations of this type except for highly ritualized language use; prayer, greetings, leave-taking, thanking etc. In actual fact, those situational syllabuses which do exist are grammatical syllabuses which make use of situations to present and practise linguistic forms.

The Notional Syllabus

The notional syllabus takes semantic knowledge as primary. It attempts to answer the question 'what do users of the language need to express?' This implies a belief in a language as a system but a system of meanings, rather than forms. It assumes that learning a language consists of learning how to mean : Such a syllabus would seek correlations between form and function. The notional syllabus attempts to define the communication needs of the learner and then to display the ways in which each communication need can be appropriately expressed.

The notional syllabus too presents problems. The specification of needs may well turn out to be global. Most learners will need to express everything in the L_2 which they can express in L_1. The notions themselves tend to overlap. The correlation between notion and form is complex. Adult utterances are frequently ambiguous or multifunctional.

The need is for a syllabus which combines the best of all the three types. It is a syllabus which gives the ideal balance between the correct production and comprehension of the linguistic forms and their appropriate use in actual communication.

The Problem of Grading

If we attempt to design syllabus a priori — on the basis of assumptions of what is needed by the learner — we assume not only the selection of items but the organization of those items into some rational order, *i.e.,* grading. The essential problem involved in grading is to distinguish what is grammatically simple from what is psychologically easy to learn. Three kinds of grading problems arise depending on the items to be graded : grammatical, situational or notional.

A grammatical syllabus takes grammatical items — in the broad sense of 'code' items : sound system, syntax and lexis — to be the units to be taught and grades them from simplest to most complex. The sound system has to be learned in its entirety, probably from the earliest stages. The learner will have to be taught to recognize, distinguish among and understand the differing meanings of the whole system. All learners will need to make statements, negate them, question others and reply to questions and so on. But these are notional categories, not grammatical.

Situational syllabuses are not syllabuses which list situations, nor are the situations graded from 'easy' to 'difficult.' In a sense all situations are equally complex. It is only in ritualized interaction that the language is predictable. What can be predicted is what people might wish to mean in a particular situation, the notions they may wish to express.

We could approach the problem of grading from a different angle. We might attempt a grading based on usefulness to the learner. This implies a thorough investigation of needs as a major input to our syllabus.

The safest advice to the teacher is to approach the task of language teaching in an a posteriori way, *i.e.,* by building small scale and short term syllabuses on the basis of the analysis of learner's errors. The ideal syllabus would be one based on a needs analysis in which language items are presented cyclically and, if graded at all, graded in a rather adhoc way which reflected both usefulness and ease of learning.

The Functional-notional Syllabus

The American sociolinguist Dell Hynes provided researchers into the functional-notional syllabus with the concept of communicative competence. Hynes maintained that a sentence must be appropriate in relation to the context in which it is used, and that speakers of a language have communicative competence — a knowledge of appropriacy — first as they have linguistic competence — a knowledge of grammar. Appropriacy to context is related to a number of situational factors, summed up by Hynes by the acronym SPEAKING : setting, participants, ends (aims and results of the communication), acts (the form and sequence of the message), key (the manner of delivery), instrumentalities (the channel of communication), norms (conduct of the participants), and genre. This approach to situation appeared to offer a more detailed model than the one presented by Halliday. A fundamental influence on the development of the functional-notional approach was the British philosopher J.L. Austin and his work *How to do Things with Words* (1962).

The functional-notional syllabus is the first manifestation of the communicative approach. After his critique of grammatical and situational syllabus, Wilkins discusses the notional syllabus in his pioneering work *Notional Syllabuses* (1976). Its starting point is the 'desired communicative capacity'. It does not ask how speakers of the language express themselves, but what it is they communicate through language. It is organized in terms of the content rather than the form of the language. In a notional syllabus it is assumed that speakers will need to express three kinds of meanings : semantico-grammatical categories (perceptions of events, processes, states and abstractions), modality, and categories of communicative function. The first task of a notional syllabus designer is to choose the types of meaning to be learned. Once this has been accomplished, he must decide by what linguistic forms these meanings are to be expressed. The notional syllabus will present an inventory of concepts and functions to be learned, together with linguistic forms by which each concept or function may be expressed, and a specification of the socio-linguistic conditions determining individual forms.

Munby presents a model for specifying communicative competence. This model enables a syllabus designer with all the relevant data at his/her disposal, to produce a 'communicative syllabus' (Munby's term for a functional-notional syllabus) appropriate to the needs of a specific learner or group of learners. It works like this. Relevant information about the identity and language of the participant (learner) is first collected and referred to the Communicative Needs Processor. This takes account of the variables that affect communication needs by organising them as parameters in a dynamic relationship to each other. Munby lists fifty four skills consisting of Wilkins' concepts, cohesive relations discussed by Halliday and Hasan, the rhetorical skills advocated by Widdowson, discourse acts outlined by Sinclair and Coulthard.

Certain advocates of communicative language teaching abandoned the path of linguistics and set off in new directions. One of the earliest attempts to chart this new direction called a process approach to language teaching was a paper by Michael Breen and Christoper Candlin published in *Applied Linguistics* (1980). They say that language learning is learning how to communicate as a member of a particular socio-cultural group. The social conventions governing language form and behavour within the group are central to the process of language learning. Language learning may be seen as a process which grows out of the interaction between learners, teachers, texts and activities. The learner's communicative abilities develop in an arena of co-operative negotiation, joint interpretation and the sharing of expression.

Lesson Plan

Name of teacher	:		Standard	:
Name of School	:		Strength	:
Subject	:	English Poetry	Duration	:
Unit	:	The Solitary Reaper	Average Age	:
Sub Unit	:	Stanzas 1 and 2	Date	:

CONTENT ANALYSIS : The poem is about a sweet song of a lonely girl reaping all by herself in a quiet field.

INSTRUCTIONAL OBJECTIVES :

GENERAL :
(1) to give to pupils an idea of poetry.
(2) to develop aesthetic sense in pupils.
(3) to help pupils appreciate the beauty of the poem.
(4) to make pupils love poetry.

SPECIFIC :
(1) to create interest in the pupils to learn the poem and recite it with proper pronunciation, stress, intonation, rhyme and rhythm.
(2) to help the students to grasp the central idea contained in the poem.
(3) to share with pupils, the mood, emotion and feeling of the poet.
(4) to help them appreciate the rhyme and rhythm.

TEACHING AIDS :
(1) a map of Scotland.
(2) a picture of a woman reaping in the field.
(3) picture of some Arabian travellers.
(4) a picture to illustrate the word 'solitary.'

PREVIOUS KNOWLEDGE :
(1) Pupils have learnt similar poems in English and in their mother tongue.
(2) They know people sing various songs at work in the fields.

Content	Specification	Learning Experience	Evaluation
Introduction	responds	Teacher asks a few questions and elicits answers T. Have you ever seen people harvesting? P. Yes. T. What do they generally do in their merry mood? P. They sing some popular folk songs.	
'The Solitary Reaper' Wordsworth (BB)	listens	Today we will learn a poem about a young girl singing while reaping alone in a field.	
Model reading by the teacher	shares the poet's mood and emotion	Teacher reads the poem with correct pronunciation, stress, intonation, rhythm and pupils listen with their books closed.	
Second reading by the teacher	associates	Teacher reads the poem a second time. Pupils listen with their texts open.	
Silent reading by the pupils	infers the mood of the poet	Pupils are directed to read the poem silently.	
Removing difficulties		Teacher removes the difficulties so that pupils can understand the poem better.	
behold see (BB)	grasps the idea	Teacher tells that the usage is archaic and gives the meaning.	
Highland– the mountain area of Scot–land (BB)	gets the idea	Teacher shows the map of Scotland and gives general idea of the place.	
lass– young girl	responds	Teacher shows the picture of a girl and asks; T. What is this? P. That is the picture of a girl. T. Is she young or old? P. She is young.	
	gets the meaning	T. Then, lass means young girl.	

melancholy strain–sad song (BB)	responds	T. Do you like songs? P. Yes. T. What kind of songs do you like? P. Sad songs.	
	gets the meaning	T. We can say melancholy strain for sad songs.	
chant–sing (BB)	responds	T. Have you been to temples? P. Yes. T. Have you seen priests performing poojas? P. Yes. T. While doing so have you seen them muttering manthras? P. Yes.	
	gets the meaning	T. Otherwise we can say that they chant manthras.	
weary–tired (BB)	responds	T. After a long journey what would you feel? P. We feel tired. T. You can say that you feel weary after a long journey.	
band – a group of people	grasps the meaning	Teacher shows the picture of a group of people and describes the meaning.	
Comprehension	responds	Teacher asks a few questions and elicits answers.	1. Who catches the attention of the poet at the beginning? 2. What kind of song was she singing? 3. Did the poet understand what she was singing?
Appreciation of the poem	locates the rhyming words	Teacher asks the pupils to pick out the words such as profound-sound.	Picks out the rhyming words from the poem.

Final reading by the teacher	identifies the poet's feeling	Teacher reads the poem with correct pronunciation, stress and intonation.	
Loud reading by the pupil	shares the poet's feeling and emotion	A few pupils are chosen at random to read the poem aloud and the teacher makes necessary corrections.	
Review	recalls	Teacher asks a few questions.	1. What impression of the song do you get? 2. Who wrote the poem? 3. To whom the reaper is compared?

ASSIGNMENT : Learn the stanzas by heart.

Lesson Plan

Name of teacher :			Standard	:
Name of School :			Duration	:
			Strength	:
Subject	:	English Prose	Age	:
Unit	:	A Day's Wait		
Sub-unit	:	Paragraph 1 to 12	Date	:

CONTENT ANALYSIS : This lesson is about a boy of nine years of age, who, on hearing that his temperature has arisen to 102°, thinks that he is going to die.

STRUCTURE : as though

NEW WORDS : shivering
ache
miserable

INSTRUCTIONAL OBJECTIVES :

GENERAL : (1) Pupil develops the four language skills — listening, speaking, reading and writing.

SPECIFIC : (1) Pupil grasps the idea contained in the passage.

(2) Pupil understands the meaning and usage of new words.

(3) Pupil grasps the new structure.

TEACHING AIDS : (1) a picture of a delighted boy.

(2) a picture of a crying woman.

(3) chart for teaching 'as though'.

(4) flannel cut-outs of new words.

PREVIOUS KNOWLEDGE : Pupils have already studied some prose lessons and are familiar with doctors and medicines.

Content	Specification	Learning Experience	Evaluation
Introduction	recalls	Teacher asks a few questions and elicits answers from the pupils.	
	responds	T. Have you ever been to a hospital? P. Yes. T. Why did you go to hospital? P. We went to a hospital to consult a doctor. T. What did the doctor do? P. He took our temperature and gave some medicines. T. What do you feel when you hear the doctor say that you have high temperature? P. We are afraid.	
A Day's Wait (BB)	listens	Today we are going to learn about a boy of nine years of age. On hearing that his temperature has risen to 102°, thinks that he is going to die. In order to understand the lesson we have to learn some structure.	
Introduction of the structure 'as though'	listens and responds	Teacher shows the picture of a delighted boy and says : T. He looks delighted.	
He looks delighted (BB)		He may have got the first prize in thc games.	
He may have got the first prize (BB)	gets the idea	T. In other words we can say that he looks delighted as though he has got the first prize in games.	

He looks delighted as though he got the first prize (BB)		T. Have you seen films? P. Yes. T. Are the films stars the real characters? P. No. T. Yes. They are not the real characters but they act as though they are real characters.	
Film stars act as though they are the real characters.	gets the idea		
establishment of the structure 'as though'	practises	(see substitution table below)	Make meaningful sentences out of the table.

He speaks slowly He speaks unsteadily	as though	he is drunk. he is weak. he is sick.

VOCABULARY	responds	T. When you take a bath early in the morning on a rainy day, what is your condition?	
shivering-trembling with cold (BB)		P. We will tremble with cold. T. In other words we can say that you will be shivering with cold.	
ache-/eik/ slow and steady pain (BB)	responds	T. If your finger has cut while sharpening the pencil what do you feel?	
	infers meaning	P. We feel pain. T. In other words we can say that your finger will ache.	
miserable– very unhappy	listens and responds	Teacher shows the picture of a dying child and asks : T. Is this child very happy?	

		P. No, he is not happy.	
	gets the meaning	T. We can say that he is miserable.	
Model reading by the teacher	identifies	Teacher reads the passage with proper pronunciation, stress and intonation.	
Silent reading by the pupils	associates	Pupils are directed to read the passage silently.	
comprehension	communication	Teacher asks a few questions to check the understanding of the pupils.	(1) What is the name of this lesson? (2) How did Schatz behave when he thought that he had only headache? (3) What did the doctor do when he came?
Final reading by the teacher	identifies	Teacher once again reads the unit with proper pronunciation, stress and intonation.	
Loud reading by the pupils	follows proper stress and intonation	A few pupils are chosen at random to read the unit aloud and the teacher makes necessary corrections.	
Review	recalls	Teacher asks a few questions to renew the unit.	(1) What is the name of the boy in the classroom? (2) What is the problem

(3) What is the temperature ature of Schatz?

ASSIGNMENT : (1) Frame meaningful sentences with

(a) miserable (b) ache

(2) Combine the sentences using 'as though'

(a) He looks frightened. He may have seen a ghost.

(b) His life was not in danger. Yet he fought hard.

Lesson Plan

Name of teacher	:		Standard	:
Name of the School	:		Strength	:
			Duration	:
Subject	:	English composition	Average Age	:
Unit	:	Free composition	Date	:
Sub-Unit	:	Story writing		

CONTENT ANALYSIS : The pupils develop the story from the given outline.

INSTRUCTIONAL OBJECTIVES :

GENERAL :
(1) to develop the expressional power of pupils.
(2) to enable them to organise the idea properly and to write in sequence.
(3) to develop an interest in extra-reading.

SPECIFIC :
(1) to enable the pupils to write a composition.
(2) to enable the pupils to understand a moral in the story.

TEACHING AIDS : Series of pictures of a crow.

PREVIOUS KNOWLEDGE : The pupils have already learned some stories and they like to hear stories.

Content	Specification	Learning Experience	Evaluation
Introduction	responds and recalls	Teacher asks a few questions and elicits answers. T. Do you like stories? P. Yes. T. Which types of stories do you like? P. I like simple stories. T. Name some of the stories which you know. P. The Lion and the Bull, the Hunter and the Ant.	
The Thirsty Crow	listens	T. Today we are going to study the story of a thirsty crow	
	observes	Teacher shows the pictures and asks questions to develop the story. T. What do you see in this picture? P. A crow is flying. T. Is it night? P. No, it is a hot day. T. How will the crow feel? P. It will feel thirsty. T. Is there any water? P. No. Teacher writes the outline of the story on the black-board.	
Outline A crow – thirsty – searches for water – sees a jar near a well – very little water – tries hard			

– fails – picks pebbles – drops them – water comes up – drinks – flies away			
Oral development	observes responses	Teacher asks the pupils to develop the story through pictures and questions.	(1) What did the crow search for? (2) Where did the crow see the jar? (3) How much water was in the jar? (4) What did the crow see near the jar? (5) How did the water rise up? (6) What is the moral behind the story?
Writing the composition	develops	Teacher asks the pupils to write the composition making use of the hints. **A Thirsty Crow** Once there was a crow. One hot day it felt very thirsty. It flew far and wide in search of water. But there was not a drop of water anywhere. At last it saw a jar near the well. It looked into the jar. There was only a little water at the bottom of the jar. It tried hard but it could not reach the bottom. It saw some pebbles near the jar. Suddenly an idea flashed in its mind. It picked up the	

		pebbles one by one and put them into the jar. The water rose up. The crow drank the water. It was happy. It cawed and flew away.
	reproduces	The moral : Where there is a will there is a way.
Correc-tion compo-sition		Teacher collects the com-position books and corrects the mistakes.

ASSIGNMENT : Develop the story from the outline.

Lesson Plan

Name of the teacher :		Standard	:
Name of the School :		Strength	:
		Duration	:
Subject	: English guided composition	Average age	:
Unit	: Letter writing	Date	:
Sub-Unit	: Personal letter		

CONTENT ANALYSIS : The form of the personal letter consists of the following parts :

1. Place and date
2. Salutation
3. Body of the letter
4. Conclusion and signature.

INSTRUCTIONAL OBJECTIVES :

1. to use the form of the letter
2. to think logically and systematically the idea
3. to use the language correctly
4. to develop the language skills.

TEACHING AIDS : A model letter

PREVIOUS KNOWLEDGE : Pupils know about two hundred common vocabulary.

Content	Specification	Learning Experience	Evaluation
Introduction	responds	Teacher asks a few questions and elicits answers T. Where do you come from? P. I come from Kollam. T. Suppose your father got an appointment in Delhi. How will you communicate? P. I will communicate through a letter. T. Do you know how to write a letter? P. No	
Personal letter	observes and responds	T. Today we are going to learn to write a letter Teacher shows a model letter and asks T. Who wrote this letter? P. The letter was written by a father to a son. T. So this is a personal letter. This is an informal letter.	
Model reading by the teacher	Identifies	Teacher reads the letter effectively with correct stress. Pupils listen	
Comprehension	responds	Teacher asks a few questions to check the general understanding of the letter 1. What did the father write at first? 2. What is there after the place and date? 3. Where is the position of place and date? 4. After place and date what is there?	

		5. Where does the body part start?	
Review	recalls	Teacher asks a few questions and elicits answers	(1) How does the salutation end? (2) How is the letter concluded? (3) Where do we put the signature?

ASSIGNMENT : Write a reply to your father asking him to send you gift.

Testing and Evaluation

Language testing is central to language teaching. It provides goals for language teaching. It monitors for both teachers and learners success in reaching the goals. Its influence on teaching is strong. It provides a methodology for experiment and investigation in both language teaching and language learning/acquisition. It is normal for teaching to be directed towards assessment, sometimes labelled examination. Discussions of language testing are typically instrumental and mechanistic concerning the how and the what. What is needed is a more humanistic account of the scope and role of language testing. What language testing does is to compel attention to the meaning of ideas in linguistics and applied linguistics. A test forces choice, removes ambiguity and reveals what has been elusive.

Many language teachers harbour a deep mistrust of tests and testers. The effect of testing on teaching and learning is known as backwash. Backwash can be harmful or beneficial. If a test is regarded as important, then preparation for it can come to dominate all teaching and learning activities. If the test content and testing techniques are at variance with the objectives of the course, then there is likely to be harmful backwash. An instance of this could be where students are following an English course which is meant to train them in the language skills necessary for university study in an English speaking country, but when the language test which they have to take in order to be admitted to a university does not test those skills directly. If the skill of writing, for example, is tested only by multiple choice items, then there is great pressure to practise such items rather than practise the skill of writing itself. This is clearly undesirable.

In modern educational practice the term 'evaluation' is used in place of 'test' or 'examination.' It implies an important change in the concept as well. Evaluation is a much more comprehensive term than either test or examination. It is concerned not only with the measurement of the extent of learning but also with determining the worth or value of that learning. The worth of any learning is judged in terms of the objectives of teaching. Thus evaluation and the teaching-learning activities are linked to a common goal — the objectives of teaching the subject. Modern evaluation is said to be objective-based.

Test and examinations are still the most widely-used tools of evaluation. However, a distinction is sometimes made between the two. A test is regarded as an attempt to see whether the things taught have been learnt, while an examination is regarded as an attempt to find out whether the pupils have attained a certain predetermined standard. A test is directly concerned with teaching while an examination is linked with an externally fixed standard of achievement. Since both tests and examinations have the same common function namely evaluation, it has become conventional to call them tests.

Tests can be used for various purposes. Some of them are to find out pupils' strengths and weaknesses and take suitable remedial measures; to judge the success or failure of the teacher's own teaching and make necessary changes in his method and strategy; to set a definite goal before the pupils to learn; to change pupils' study habits and improve the quality of teaching; to select pupils for promotion to the next higher class or to award certificates; to assess the quality of the staff and the effectiveness of the activities of the school.

The quality of a test is usually judged on the basis of objectivity, validity, reliability and administrability. A test is said to be objective when its scoring is free from the subjective judgement of the examiner. It is valid when it actually tests the objective it aims to test. Reliability of a test is determined by its consistency in results. A test that gives different results on different occasions is not reliable. Administrability relates to the actual giving of the test. The best test in the world would be of little value if it cannot be given properly.

Oral and Written Tests

A test may be either oral or written. Since listening and speaking are two major objectives of teaching English, oral tests have an important role. It may not always be practical to have oral tests at public examinations. But that should not reduce their importance in the class tests. With a little bit of planning it is even possible to have oral tests in annual promotion examinations. This would provide a strong incentive for the pupils to learn the aural-oral skills, and for the teachers to teach them. An oral test is a quick and effective device for testing pupils' progress and difficulties.

Written tests are by far the most popular testing tools in our schools. They can be used to test most of the objectives of teaching English. Depending upon the length of the answer and the objectivity in scoring the tests are generally placed in four major types — objective type, very short answer type, short answer type and essay type. Each of these types has certain advantages and disadvantages. Besides, one type may test a particular objective better than another.

Objective-type Tests

In recent times the objective-type tests have become very popular. Various quiz competitions and intelligence tests have increased their popularity even with people who are not directly concerned with education. The objective type test derives its name from the objectivity in scoring. There is only one correct answer to such a test. In most cases the answer is given along with the test. The candidate is simply required to indicate the correct answer with a tick or a number. The subjective judgement of the examiner cannot vitiate the scoring. Some of the popular types of objective type test are multiple-choice type, matching type, true-false type, completion type etc. The objective type tests can cover large area of the syllabus in relatively short time. They can be scored easily and effectively. They can evaluate only certain limited aspects of language skills. They can be positively harmful, encouraging blind guessing and fragmentary learning of language items.

Essay-type Tests

The essay-type tests are considered least satisfactory. They are often subjected to severe criticism. In language, the essay type tests seem indispensable. They appear to be the only valid tests of communicative competence in writing.

Short-answer Type Tests

Short-answer type tests require short answers. The length of the answer in most cases is a matter of subjective judgement. The short-answer type tests combine the advantages objectivity and wider coverage of the syllabus of the objective-type tests. They seem to be a happy compromise between objective-type tests and essay type tests.

The Unit-test

Testing is implicit in teaching. Annual and terminal examinations are held to evaluate pupils' progress over a period of time. These examinations are usually held when the entire syllabus or a considerable part of it has been taught. They cannot provide much guidance for taking remedial measures or for assessing the effectiveness of the method of teaching. It is therefore desirable to have periodic tests at more frequent intervals. For this the entire syllabus can be broken down into manageable units of some related topics or lessons. A test can be given as soon as each unit is completed. Such tests are called unit tests. These tests may last only one lesson-period of forty to forty-five minutes. They may be given in usual classroom conditions. An imaginative planning of unit tests will prove very meaningful.

Remedial Teaching

A remedial test is not an end in itself. It is only a means to an end, the end being the pupils' mastery of the unit taught. Teaching, evaluation and remedial measures are the three classic steps in any teaching-learning process. If the teacher stops with the test, the entire process would remain incomplete. The logical step after the step is to take necessary remedial measures in the light of the pupils' performance in the test. The aim of this step is not just revision of earlier work but systematic treatment of pupils' learning problems. A remedy should be based on an identification of the malady and its causes. The teacher has to study the test results closely and sort out the serious errors. Pupils' errors may be due to the pull of the mother tongue, over-learning, false analogy or over-generalisation of a rule, inherent difficulty of a particular item, defective teaching. Having discovered the cause of the error, the teacher has to devise a strategy to deal with it. The follow-up measures may involve changing the teaching method, reteaching some of the previous lessons, arranging tutorials, or even dividing the weaker pupils into separate groups for more intense case.

Proficiency Tests

Proficiency tests are designed to measure people's ability in a language regardless of any training they may have had in the language. The content of a proficiency test is based on a specification of what candidates have to be able to do in the language in order to be considered proficient. In the case of some proficiency tests, 'proficient' means having sufficient command of the language for a particular purpose. An example of this would be a test designed to discover whether someone can function successfully as a United Nations translator. For some other tests the concept of proficiency is more general.

Achievement Tests

Most teachers are unlikely to be responsible for proficiency tests. It is much more probable that they will be involved in the preparation and use of achievement tests. Achievement tests are directly related to language courses. Their purpose is to establish how successful individual students, groups of students, or the courses themselves have been in achieving objectives. They are of two types : final achievement tests and progress achievement tests. Final achievement tests are those administered at the end of a course of study. They may be written and administered by ministries of education, official examining boards, or by members of teaching institutions. The content of these tests must be related to the courses with which they are concerned. Progress achievement tests are intended to measure the progress that students are making. One way of measuring progress would be repeatedly to administer final achievement tests. Progress tests based on short term objectives will fit well with what has been taught.

Diagnostic Tests

Diagnostic tests are used to identify students' strengths and weaknesses. They are intended primarily to ascertain what further teaching is necessary. At the level of broad language skills this is reasonably straight forward. We can be fairly confident of our ability to create tests that will tell us that a student is particularly weak in, say, speaking as opposed to reading in a language. Indeed existing proficiency tests may often prove adequate for this purpose. Diagnostic tests could be extremely useful for individual instruction or self-instruction. Learners would be shown where gaps exist in their command of the language and could be directed to sources of information, exemplification and practice. The ready availability of relatively inexpensive computers with very large memories may change the situation of the lack of good diagnostic tests. Well-written computer programmes would ensure that the learner spent no more time than was absolutely necessary to obtain the desired information.

Placement Tests

Placement tests are intended to provide information which will help to place students at the stage or in the part of the teaching programme most appropriate to their abilities. Typically they are used to assign students to classes at different levels. They can be bought but this is not to be recommended unless the institution concerned is quite sure that the test being considered suits its particular teaching programme. No one placement test will work for every institution. The placement tests which are most successful are those constructed for particular situations. They depend on the identification of the key features at different levels of teaching in the institution. They are tailor-made rather than bought off the peg.

Direct versus Indirect Testing

Testing is said to be direct when it requires the candidate to perform precisely the skill which we wish to measure. If we want to know how well candidates can write compositions, we get them to write compositions. If we want to know how well they pronounce a language; we got them to speak. The tasks, and the texts which are used, should be as authentic as possible. Direct testing is easier to carry out when it is intended to measure the productive skills of speaking and writing. The very acts of speaking and writing provide us with information about the candidate's ability. With listening and reading it is necessary to get candidates not only to listen or read but also to demonstrate that they have done this successfully. Direct testing is relatively straight forward. Atleast in the case of the productive skills, the assessment and interpretation of pupils' performance is also quite straight forward. There is likely to be a helpful backwash effect.

Indirect testing attempts to measure the abilities which underlie the skills in which we are interested. An example of indirect testing is Lado's proposed method of testing pronunciation ability by a paper and pencil test in which the candidate has to identify pairs of words which rhyme with each other. Indirect testing seems to offer the possibility of testing a representative sample of a finite number of abilities which underlie a potentially indefinitely large number of manifestations of them. The main problem with indirect tests is that the relationship between performance on them and performance of the skills in which we are usually more interested tends to be rather weak in strength and uncertain in nature.

Discrete Point *versus* Integrative Testing

Discrete point testing refers to the testing of one element at a time, item by item. This might involve a series of items each testing a particular grammatical structure. Integrative testing requires the candidate to combine many language elements in the completion of a task. This might involve writing a composition, making notes while listening to a lecture, taking a dictation or completing a close passage. Discrete point tests will almost always be indirect, while integrative tests will tend to be direct. However, some integrative testing methods, such as the clozeprocedure, are indirect.

The Cloze Test

The cloze test is based on the Gestalt theory in psychology. This theory holds that the human mind tends to see things in their entirety. This tendency leads the mind to fill any gaps in a pattern and see it as a whole. For example, if a person is shown a circle with a small gap in the drawing, he would not see the gap and would take it as a complete circle. This tendency also functions in language use. When we read we do not usually see the printing mistake in a familiar word. We may even supply a missing word without being aware of the omission. A person can do this when he understands the passage being read and has acquired the structural patterns in it as part of his reflex behaviour. The test therefore requires the candidates to supply the missing words in a given passage. This is not exactly like the usual fill-in-the-blank tests. In this test the words for deletion are not deliberately selected by the item-writer. He simply decides that every nth word in the passage will be deleted, and accordingly deletes the words mechanically. This mechanical deletion of words eliminates any scope for subjective judgement of the item-writer. At the same time no clue is provided to the candidate as to the kind of words deleted. The difficulty level of the test depends on the frequency of the words deleted. Since the test is based on the tendency of the mind to achieve completion or closure, it is called Cloze test. A Cloze test may be scored either for the exact words used by the original writer of the passage, or for acceptable equivalents. It tests both comprehension and expression. It demands greater proficiency in the language on the part of the candidate.

Thinking

There is no mystery about what it means to think, and nothing complicated about all the different words used to describe thoughtful activities. There are many complaints from inside and outside schools about the quality of student thinking. These complaints are venerable and unanswerable. Parents of generations have been convinced that their children are not taught as well as they were. But the complaints rest on exactly the same assumptions about thinking as those of the educators and theorists who are trying to do something about thinking in schools. They assume that special things have to go on in the brain in order for particular kinds of thinking to take place, and that instruction is the only means by which people can come to think better.

Frank Smith views that thinking is 'the business of the brain.' This concept is close to one of the dictionary definitions of thinking — 'the exercise of the mind.' We regard the brain as an instrument and the mind as its product. Do ideas exist in the mind or the brain? Is the 'mind' a different 'level' of the brain, an emergent property of the brain, or a higher level of neural organization? Is the mind a convenient but misleading fiction for what are essentially and uniquely physical processes in the brain? These questions are unanswerable because the distinction between mind and brain is semantic. Words are used according to tradition, convention, idiom and style. Words are not evidence of ultimate truth. The fact that language makes a distinction does not mean that a distinction actually exists beyond our own perceptions. The difference between mind and brain is purely idiomatic and stylistic. The brain is what brain surgeons operate on, the chunk of physical substance in the skull. We tell people to use their brains, not their minds. Advertisers and propagandists manipulate our minds. We keep things in mind but have brain power.

We rarely give ourselves credit for the amount and quality of our thinking. We accuse ourselves of acting without thinking. Thinking is commonly regarded as an occasional mental chore, performed when necessity arises but not a regular occupation of the brain. But the brain is thinking all the time. There can be very few moments of the day when our brain is not busy categorizing, inferring, solving problems, deciding and engaging in other enterprises that are supposed to be components of thinking. Thinking is commonplace and usually effortless, inconspicuous, and effective. Thinking is the way the brain arranges our daily affairs, the way we cope.

The view is current, in scientific research and popular educational theorizing, that the brain is an information-processing device, functioning only under the press of immediate circumstances to seek to organize, retrieve, and utilize information. Learning is regarded as the acquisition of information; memory, its recovery; and thinking, its manipulation. The brain is more like an artist than a machine. It constantly creates realities, actual and imaginary. It examines alternatives, spins stories, and thrives on experience. It picks up huge amounts of information in our journey through life. Knowledge is a by-product of experience, and experience is what thinking makes possible.

Perception

Perception is decision-making. The brain has no direct contact with the outside world. Secluded in the dark and silent vault of the skull, the brain has no sensitivity of its own, and no direct awareness of its situation in the world. The brain's only connection with the outside world is through arrays of nerve fibres radiating to the eyes, ears, skin, and other receptive organs. The eyes are not windows on the world. We do not see what is in front of our eyes, but what we think is in front of our eyes. Nothing in the world announces itself to us. We have only to think of the way our apprehensions rule our perceptions when we are alone at night, in unfamiliar surroundings, or when our nervous expectations have been primed by a mecabre book or movie. The brain can be mistaken in the perceptual decisions that it makes. It is rarely reluctant to make perpetual decisions. It decides and creates so efficiently that we are seldom aware of all the thinking that is going on every time we see, hear, smell, taste or touch anything that we recognize.

The brain makes endless decisions involving behaviour. We decide to get up at a particular time, we decide to dress, and how to dress, and what to have for breakfast, where to go first, and how to get there and so on. Every step along the way during the day the brain plans, organizes, anticipates, categorizes, chooses, infers, solves problems, determines relationships, and makes decisions. Life would be a shambles without constant thought of the most complex kind, even among children.

We are prone to mistakes quite often. There are occasions when we cannot make up our mind. There are no generalizable decision-making (perception) skills. Decisions depend upon circumstances. Making better decisions about particular matters or states of affairs requires more experience. Willingness to make decisions on particular occasions involves personal considerations, not cognitive strategies.

Problem-solving

Our brains are constantly solving problems. Everytime we learn or remember or make sense of something, we solve a problem. In order to learn language, an infant must make sense of the contexts in which language occurs. We have all been solving problems of this kind since childhood, usually without awareness of what we are doing. Confronted by an insoluble problem, we are stymied, baffled, uncertain about what to do next.

The term problem-solving is broad and imprecise. There is no one category of events in the world that can be called problems. What is a problem for one might not be a problem for others. And behaviour that solves one problem might not solve another. There can be no general class of solutions. The difficulty with many of the problems is the inability to find an appropriate way to think about it. We do not know enough about what we are trying to think about. We lack knowledge rather than skills. Often the problem is 'other people'. The difficulty is changing their behaviour. Generalized instruction is not going to make us better at solving any of these problems. We need more experience of the particular kind of issue or person we are dealing with, and better understanding of our own habits.

Reasoning

Reasoning is not a unique, clearly distinguishable mental activity. It is not word with a unique, distinguishable application. Sometimes it is used synonymously with thinking in general. In fact 'reasoning' is a common definition of thinking. Reasoning sometimes involves justifying a conclusion already made sometimes, persuading another person to accept a conclusion. It can be an explanation of the past or an argument about the future. It attempts to tie thoughts or actions together in an unbroken series of links.

No general criteria can be presented for what makes a good argument, an acceptable rationale or appropriate reasoning. Ability to reason comes with understanding what one is endeavoring to reason about. There are no general rules that will make anyone an expert reasoner. There can be no hard-and-fast rules of reasoning. Reasoning is often used to justify a position rather than to achieve the most appropriate one. Reasoning can be used to justify any desired position. The links in a chain of reasoning are never complete. There are always missing premises that have to be filled in by the listener or reader if reasoning is to be 'followed'. No one has the patience or the knowledge, to specify or examine every consideration upon which an argument is based.

Reasoning is not an exotic or uncommon activity. It is something else the brain does all the time. We do not usually behave unthinkingly. When we do things, we do them for a reason. We become aware of reasoning when we run into difficulty.

Higher-order Thinking

Higher-order thinking is not in common use. It does not crop up in daily conversation. It is not to be found in standard dictionaries. The term occurs most frequently in psychological and educational parlance. It is a status term. Like all status terms, it discriminates. And like many forms of discrimination, it is based on purely imaginary distinctions.

Higher-order thinking is presumed to be a superior mix of high-value attributes or components, such as planning, predicting, monitoring, evaluating and questioning. It often includes an executive function that is able to take charge and exercise leadership. It is presumed to be more complex, more recondite, requiring more attention and a superior brain. But all the supposed elements of higher-order thinking are in fact common place. They are a continuous and intrinsic part of everyday thought. They only look difficult when pulled out of everyday contexts. We are planning and predicting every moment of our lives. We all monitor and evaluate, the consequences of our own thinking and the thinking of other people. Everybody questions. There is no skill of questioning. We think impulsively or compulsively.

Easy and Difficult Thinking

Thinking is usually easy, a commonplace affair. We think all the time, without effort, without awareness, and usually without gross error. Thinking is easy and effective when two fundamental requirements are met; the need to understand what we are thinking about and the brain itself in charge, in control of its affairs. Thinking becomes difficult and inefficient when the brain loses control. Contrived thinking goes against the predominant tendency of thought.

When thinking is done for ourselves, we have no trouble with it. It is only difficult and inefficient thinking that one becomes aware of, in oneself and others. In consequence it is widely believed that thinking is difficult and inefficient.

Private and Personal Thinking

Thinking done for totally personal reasons, usually has secure roots in our own intentions, values, considerations and desires. We usually know where we are coming from and where we want to get to. Our thoughts can range without the inhibition of other people's possible reaction. The business of the brain is the construction of realities.

There is much fantasy in private thought. Wishful thinking about the future may constitute detailed planning or rehearsal for coming possibilities. Rueful thinking can often be preparation for similar circumstances in future. Both wishful and rueful thinking can be experiences from which we learn.

Personal thinking can be highly ideosyncratic. It is self-oriented, inquisitive and expressive. It is what gets us through life in our own way. Social thinking tends to be more consensus, other-oriented. It has more constraints. Teachers, colleagues, officials, family members and friends influence how we think and what we think about. They evaluate the consequences of our thought. We may not think that we are making a mistake, but other people may. Other people may not think their thinking is defective, but we do. Questioning our own belief is difficult. Children change their mind all the time as they learn about the world. But as we grow older, we develop an investment in the way we see the world. One of the major functions of thinking is to create an identity for ourselves.

Remembering

In education, reading and writing are not always assumed to presuppose thinking. Nor are remembering understanding and learning. These behaviours are often discussed as if they are quite different from thinking, mutually exclusive, to be studied in different contexts and taught separately. These behaviours do involve thinking. They are aspects of thinking. They can be regarded as the byproducts of thinking. We remember, understand and learn all the time as we think.

The brain is continuously remembering without effort or conscious awareness. We remember, with remarkable precision, exactly what we need to remember, when we need to remember. When we wake-up in the morning we remember who we are and where we are. We remember what we have planned for the day. We remember to have breakfast. We remember to dress before we leave home. But we do not remember everything all the time. Memory lets us down sometimes. We cannot always remember what we want to remember.

In general we remember all the time, without difficulty, when remembering is part of the flow of events in which we are involved, when we can make sense what we are doing. Remembering is easy when it is not a particular focus of attention. We remember best when we are engaged in an activity that is interesting and meaningful to us, when the brain is in charge of its affairs. Remembering is difficult when it becomes a deliberate activity.

Remembering cannot be separated from thinking. Remembering is simply thinking about the past. It is indistinguishable from thinking. Whenever we think about the past, we remember. Whenever we project our thoughts into the future, we bring thoughts about the past with us. Remembering is simply the past tense of thinking.

Understanding

Understanding is not an unusual condition for anyone to be in. It is the opposite of confusion. Most of the time we are not confused. Infants seen remarkably competent at making sense of the world; they rarely look bewildered. We wake in the morning and we are not confused. We set out to do what we planned to do without confusion. Understanding is something that everyone is capable of, that everyone demonstrates, in most situations and most of the time, without special exercises or instruction. It is not a passive activity. We do not wait for things to make sense to us. Understanding takes us beyond the known to the new. It makes experience possible. Ofcourse it fails us occasionally. Failure to understand is much more likely to be a case of inadequate experience. We all have intellectual 'disabilities' that are constant sources of confusion, impenetrable to our comprehensions, no matter how hard we try to make sense of them.

Like remembering, understanding is easy when it is not a particular source of attention, when we are engaged in something that is interesting, meaningful and natural to us, when the brain is in charge of its own affairs. Understanding is difficult in contrived circumstances. Experimental psychologists have not studied understanding as much as they have studied remembering or learning.

It is not possible to separate understanding from thinking as mental processes. The brain is not doing different things when we understand and when we think. Understanding is thinking. One's understanding may change in the course of one's thinking. Thinking proceeds from understanding to understanding. Understanding is simply the present tense of thinking.

Learning

No one has ever tried to catalogue how much individuals learn in a lifetime, or even in a single day. The learning that we do is vast. Learning is commonplace, continual, effortless and inconspicuous. Everything we can remember we must have learned. Learning is not difficult. It does not require deliberate motivation. Most of the time we learn without knowing that we are learning. The moment we find ourselves in a situation where we are learning nothing, we are bored. Boredom means we know so much about what is going on, or understand so little of it, that there is nothing to be learned.

We learn so that we conform to the identity we construct for ourselves. Language defines the way we see ourselves as being, and children learn to talk exactly like the kind of person they see themselves as being. Quite unwittingly, without practice or effort, they learn to speak precisely the way their friends talk. Teaching children to speak differently is a complete waste of time. What we learn is how we see ourselves, how other people persuade us to see ourselves, not only in the way we talk, but in the way we dress, groom and ornament ourselves, in the way we organize the world, in our beliefs and attitudes. Every child learns a culture, which is the way we all define ourselves.

Learning is easy when it is part of the flow of events in which we are involved, when we can make sense what we are doing, when the brain is in charge of its own affairs. Learning is easy when it is not a particular focus of attention, when it happens in the course of doing something else. We learn best when we are engaged in an activity that is interesting and meaningful to us, where our past experience is relevant.

It is contrived learning that has been studied most by experimental psychologists. Contrived learning is the basis of psychology's laws of learning that have most influenced education. Learning is easiest when external control is relaxed, when individuals are permitted to take charge of their own learning.

Learning is not something that is done separately from thinking. Inferring, concluding, deciding and solving problems are inseparable from learning. The learning and the conclusion occur together.

Learning without thinking would be pointless. Learning is inevitable. It is commonplace.

Learning and thinking are not carried on consecutively, or even simultaneously by different parts of the brain. We learn in the course of thinking. We not only learn about situations, we learn how we feel about situations. Learning is the aspect of thinking that carries us into the future. Thinking is always oriented to the future.

Glossary

a posteriori : an artificial language based on elements from one or more natural language.

a priori : an artificial language composed entirely of invented elements.

accent : features of pronunciation that identify where a person is from, regionally or socially. Technically distinct from dialect since a standard dialect may be pronounced with a regional accent.

acccptancc : acknowledgement by an educated native speaker of a language that a sentence or other linguistic unit conforms to the norms of the language.

achievement test : instrument designed to measure what a person has learned within a given period of time of a known syllabus or course of instruction.

acquisition : the process of picking up a language without formal instruction and without a sustained conscious effort to learn the language. Acquisition usually occurs as a result of highly motivated exposure to the language in use plus the need and opportunity to communicate in the language.

anaphoric reference : the use of a word or phrase to refer back to a word or group of words previously mentioned.

aphasia : loss of speech or of understanding of language, owing to brain damage.

appropriacy	: acknowledgement by an educated native speaker of a language that a sentence or other linguistic unit is suitable or possible in a given social situation.
aptitude	: innate language learning ability.
artificial language	: a language which has been invented to serve some particular purpose.
attainment tests	: language tests which seek to discover information about the language abilities of the learners. Unlike achievement tests they are not restricted to testing what learners have been taught.
audio aids	: aids such as radios, record players, tape recorders and language laboratories which help the learners by exposing them to the spoken language.
audio-lingual approach	: an approach to language teaching based on listening and then speaking. It relies heavily on oral imitation, memorization and drills designed to produce correct language habits.
audio-visual aids	: aids such as televisions, films and video equipment which allow the learners to see a situation as well as listen to the language used in it.
aural comprehension	: activities which involve the learners listening to and responding to spoken language.
authentic materials	: materials such as newspaper articles, brochures, train tickets, letters, advertisements, recording of the news, airport announcements etc. which were originally used in real situations and were not designed for use in language teaching. Such materials are used in the classroom to expose the learners to language in real use.

authentic tasks	:	responses to spoken or written material which would be natural to real participants in a real situation. For example, learners in a classroom who read a text telling them what is on at the theatres in a city and then decide which theatre to go to.
background speakers	:	home-users of a language that is not the official medium of the speech community.
backwash effect	:	the effect that the nature of the final examination has on the teaching and learning during a course. An examination which focuses on tests of grammatical knowledge is likely to lead to the teaching and learning of grammatical knowledge in courses preparing candidates for the examination, whereas a communicative examination is likely to encourage communicative approaches and activities in the classroom.
basic English	:	a modified natural language (rather than an artificial language) promoted by C.K. Ogden in the early 1930s (BASIC being an acronym for British American Scientific International Commercial)
behaviourist theories	:	theories based on the assumption that language learning is a process of habit formation relying on correct imitation and frequent repetition.
berlitz	:	the name associated with many language schools world-wide employing a particular method of language teaching in which the target language only is used in class and all the teachers are native speakers.
bilingual	:	a person able to speak a second language as well as if it was his or her first language or a person with two first languages.

British Council : a government-funded but independent organization concerned to foster interest in British culture, including both English language and literature.

case grammar : an approach to grammatical analysis devised by Charles Fullmore in the late 1960s within the generative grammar framework but emphasizing certain semantic relationships.

C.D.A. : critical discourse analysis analyses how linguistic choices in texts are used to maintain and create social inequalities.

clinical linguistics : either the application of linguistics to a medical setting involving language disorders or the practice of professionals such as speech therapists working in those areas.

cloze test : a test of language proficiency in which the learner has to fill in blanks in a continuous passage. There are many variations on the cloze test. The basic type involves the setter selecting a passage and then deleting every nth word.

codification : producing systematic statements of the rules and conventions of a language variety. The variety usually chosen for codification is the standard dialect and the act of codifying increases its acceptance as the standard.

cognitive approaches : approaches to language teaching which involve the learners thinking about the language and working out rules from examples.

co-herence : the linking together of consecutive utterances in accordance with the function of the utterances. Thus an invitation followed by an acceptance or a generalization followed by an example would be coherent whereas a factual enquiry followed by an anecdote would not be coherent.

cohesion : the logical linking of consecutive or related utterances.

collocation : words which are frequently used together are said to be collocates. Thus, 'pillow,' 'bed,' and 'sheet' are collocates but 'cushion' and 'bed' are not.

communicative activities : activities designed to get learners to use the language for communication rather than for the language practice. The main aims of these activities are to help the learners to gain confidence, to become more fluent and to acquire language through exposure and use.

communicative approaches : approaches to teaching EFL which stress the importance of learning through using the language and which give the learners frequent opportunities to interact with each other and with the teacher in 'natural' situations.

communicative competence : a measure of a learner's ability to achieve successful communication in the language he is learning.

communication gap : the disparity in knowledge and experience that exists between people involved in communication with each other. The wife who asks her husband 'who won?' the doctor who asks his patient 'how do you feel today?' the policeman who directs a motorist to 'Turn right at the cinema,' are doing so because of a communication gap. Much of the interaction between the teacher and the learners in the classroom is extremely artificial because there is no communication gap between the participants. (Notes : some books use the term 'information gap' instead of 'communication gap.'

competence : the unconscious or implicit knowledge of language that the native speaker has, and which is the object of linguistics to systematize in rules.

connotation : the association which a word or group of words has for a particular language user or community of language users.

construct : a theory of linguistic knowledge or ability that may be operationalized in a language test.

context : the situation in which an utterance is used. To understand the context you need to have information about the setting, the topic and the roles and relationships of the participants in the interaction. The context is often referred to as the situational context to differentiate it from the linguistic context or cotext. Some writers use 'context' to refer to both the situational environment and the linguistic environment.

context of situation : a term deriving from the work of the anthropologist Bronislaw Malinowski referring to the relationship between external world features such as place and participants and language utterance.

contracted forms : Verb forms which are shortened in informal speech. *e.g.,* : I've, she's, they'd etc.

contrastive analysis : comparing two different languages to discover in what ways they are the same, similar and different in order to predict likely learner errors or explain discovered errors.

contrastive linguistics : a method of exploring structural similarities and differences between languages, important in historical linguistics and formerly influential in language teaching.

controlled exercises : a practice exercise in which the learners are told exactly what to do and how to do it. It is hoped that nearly all the learners will get nearly all the exercises right and will therefore develop correct habits and gain useful knowledge about the language.

corpus linguistics : a use of the computer to collect a large sample of language both spoken and written for purposes of description.

correction : the putting right of a particular instance of language use which is considered faulty.

cotext : the language which is used before and after a particular utterance being referred to. This is often known as the linguistic environment or the linguistic context of the utterance.

creation : the ability of a language learner to produce utterances which he has never heard or read and therefore cannot possibly have remembered and reproduced. The learner creates by making use of subconscious generalisations based upon his exposure to the language in use.

creole : a language which has developed as a result of a combination between local languages and an outside language and which has become the native language of a community of its speakers.

critical applied linguistics : a judgemental approach by some applied linguists to 'normal' applied linguistics as the grounds that it is not concerned with the transformation of society.

critical discourse : an approach to language use as the manifestation of political ideology.

cue cards : (1) cards shown to learners to guide their responses in a drill.

(2) cards given to participants in a role play or simulation to tell them who they and not what they are going to do.

curriculum : the total teaching programme of a school or educational system. Sometimes used synonymously with syllabus.

cyclical syllabus : a syllabus in which each particular aspect of the language occurs many times.

declension : a tradition term for a class of nouns, adjectives or pronouns; the usual contemporary linguistic term is word-class.

deficit grammar : the grammar of those whose language development is said to be incomplete.

deductive : referring to the process of consciously working out rules of the language from an analysis of the samples of the language.

denotation : the actual thing referred to by a word or group of words as opposed to ideas or feelings associated with the word.

descriptive linguistics: the approach which sets out to describe the facts of language usage as they are at a particular period of time.

diachronic : the dimension of linguistic investigation which studies the historical development of languages.

diagnostic test : a test designed to discover what a learner or group of learners can do and cannot do in the language. Such a test would be used at the beginning of a course to provide information on which schemes of work could be based or during a course to provide information relating to a particular area of

		language scheduled to be taught to the learners.
dialect	:	a regional or social variety of a language, frequently used to refer to any variety which is not the standard. Dialects can be regional or social.
dialogue	:	a conversation presented to the learners to exemplify certain aspects of the spoken language and then used as the basis of practice activities.
dictation	:	an exercise or test involving the learners writing down the language which is spoken to them. It is claimed that what the learners write reveals evidence about many aspects of their language ability.
diglossia	:	a situation in which two distinct varieties of a language are used in a speech community for quite distinct purposes.
direct method	:	an approach to language teaching emphasising the spoken language.
discourse	:	language used in a real situation for real purposes. In other words language as social behaviour. Such a use of language invariably involves interaction and the combining and relating of utterances.
discourse analysis	:	the study of how a language actually works in real situations. This involves not only studying the phonology, grammar and vocabulary of the language but also of the ways in which people interact and the ways in which they use language to achieve situational purposes.
discrete point tests	:	tests which aim to provide very specific information about learners' abilities in particular skills or in particular language areas. This type of test focuses on one item

		at a time and therefore tests knowledge of it rather than ability to use it in real situations.
discriminatory language	:	racist, sexist etc. language which is hurtful to disempowered groups in society.
drills	:	language practice exercises designed to give the learners many opportunities to use the correct forms and thus to establish correct habits. They are designed to demonstrate the regularity of the rule they exemplify and to fix it through repetition in the learner's mind.
dysarthria	:	speech abnormalities caused by neuromuscular disorders.
dyslexia	:	partial inability to read, characterised by associative learning difficulty.
ebonics	:	a term used for the variety of English spoken by Afro-Americans also known as Black English.
educational linguistics	:	applied linguistics focusing on educational problems.
EAP (English for Academic Purposes)	:	EAP courses are designed for students taking or about to take academic courses using English as the medium of instruction. They are usually specially designed to help the participants to understand and use those aspects of English which they will need during their academic courses.
EFL (English as a Foreign Language)	:	English learned by people from a community where English is not normally used. Thus an Italian, a Russian, an Argentinian or a German learning English would be learning it as a foreign language.
elementary level	:	the lowest of the levels in which EFL learners are placed on entry to a course. Classes at this level include learners ranging

		from complete beginners to those who have picked up enough English to communicate inaccurately but effectively in everyday situations.
EOP (English for Occupational Purposes)	:	EOP courses are designed for people who need to learn English in order to help them carry out their job. Usually these courses are planned to cater for the specific needs of the participants. Thus an EOP course designed for pilots would be very different from one for hotel managers or customs officials.
error	:	a term used in second language teaching to refer to a non-trivial deviation from the target language. Errors are usually caused by false generalizations about the language by the learner. They are an inevitable and essential part of language learning. Many such errors are developmental and disappear as the learner gains more exposure to the language in use.
error analysis	:	a procedure typically used in conjuction with contrastive analysis to determine the extent of transfer from the first to the target language.
ESL (English as a Second Language)	:	English learned by people from communities where English is not the native language but where it is used for various social purposes such as education, commerce, government and religion. Thus an Indian, a Nigerian, a Jamaican, a Fijian or a Kenyan learning English would be learning it as a second language.
ESP (English for Specific Purposes or English for English Purposes)	:	ESP courses are designed for people who are designed for people who are learning English so that they will be able to use it in particular situations such as on a holiday,

in their job, in their training or on academic courses.

examples	:	utterances provided by a teacher, a text-book, a tape etc., in order to illustrate specific language points to learners.
exposure	:	all the language which the learner hears or reads.
extensive reading/ listening	:	reading or listening to fairly lengthy texts without necessarily achieving a hundred percent concentration or comprehension. The main aims are to increase the learners' exposure to language in use, to develop language skills and to stimulate motivation through a sense of enjoyment and achievement.
false beginners	:	those learners who seem to be complete beginners because of their inability to use the language they are learning but who have had previous learning experiences of the language.
first language	:	a person's first language is the one he/she learned first as a child and which he/she has continued to use. It is often referred to as L_1.
fluency	:	the ability to use a language spontaneously and confidently and without undue pauses and hesitations.
fossilization	:	fossilization occurs when a learner's use of the target language ceases to develop and therefore his errors become permanent. This usually happens when the learner has attained his/her inner goal of easy communication in everyday face to face situations and there is no longer any real motivation for further development.

function : the use of a language form either in other parts of the system or more generally in situation.

functional approach : an approach to language teaching which stresses the purposes for which expressions are used. Thus instead of teaching the structure of English, a course based on a functional approach would teach how to express agreement, how to decline an invitation, how to give directions, how to ask for information etc.

functional linguistics : a linguistic theory taking account of verbal interaction and therefore less abstract than generative linguistics.

generalisations : assumptions about patterns of the language made by the learners as a result of his exposure to it. For example, many elementary learners make the false generalisation that the past simple tense is always formed by adding -ed to the verb and make such errors as X buyed Y. These generalisations are made unconsciously as a result of the brain processing a number of similar utterances. Making such generalisations is an important part of language learning and is the basis of first language acquisition. The learner revises his generalisations as he receives more information form the language he is exposed to and from reactions to the language he uses himself.

genre : type of spoken or written discourse or text recognised as distinct by members of a Speech community.

genuine text : a continuous passage of written or spoken language originally used to achieve real communication but subsequently used in

		the classroom as a source of exposure to language in use for the learners. Many books use the term 'authentic material' with the same meaning.
global tests	:	tests designed to assess learners' overall language ability rather than to assess particular skills. Cloze tests and dictation tests are the most frequently used global tests.
graded readers	:	books written or simplified so as to be suitable for use as extensive reading material for particular levels of learners.
grading	:	the staging or arranging of teaching material according to some predetermined order.
grammar-translation method	:	a method in which the learner is taught the grammar of the target language and is asked to use the rules he has learned to help him translate from the target language into his native language and vice versa.
guided exercises	:	practice exercises in which the learners are told what to do and then are given advice on how to do it.
HRT	:	high-rise tone, associated with a shift in English intonation patterns, observed among young people in New Zealand and Australia.
humanistic approaches	:	approaches to language teaching which stress the importance of treating the learners as individual human beings and require the teacher to be a sympathetic counsellor/guide/friend rather than an authority and instructor.
illocutionary act	:	the purposes for which an utterance is made.

inductive	:	referring to the process of gaining generalisations about the language as a result of practising sentences which exemplify them.
input	:	the language gained from exposure which is available to the brain for language processing.
instances	:	utterances used in real discourse.
intensive reading/ listening	:	reading or listening to a short text with as much concentration and understanding as possible.
interaction	:	communication between people involving the use of language.
interference	:	the negative influence of one language while learning another language. Approximately ten to fifteen percent of L_2 errors are caused by such interference.
inter language	:	the language spoken by a learner of a second or foreign language. It is called an inter language because it is felt to be in between the learner's first language and the language he is learning. As the learner progresses his inter language moves further away from the first language and closer to the language that is being learned. However, the learner still retains features which are peculiar to the inter-language and which have no apparent connection with the first language or the language he is learning.
intonation	:	the rise and fall of the voice used to indicate the functions of an utterance.
L_1	:	the learner's first language.
L_2	:	a language being learned which is not the learner's first language, *i.e.*, a second or a foreign language.

language assessment : the ambition to develop explicit linguistic understanding in the secondary school.

language death : the point at which there are no living speakers of a language.

language laboratory : a room where learners can listen to and respond to spoken language on tape. Each learner has his own tape recorder and earphones and works at his or her speed.

language shock : the fear of making errors when using a foreign language. Some learners are so afraid of being humiliated that they are reluctant to use the language at all. Such learners need confidence rather than correction. Role-play, simulation and other communication activities can help by focusing their attention on content and communication rather than expression.

learner-centred approaches : approaches to language teaching based on the needs and interests of the learners rather than on a fixed syllabus or course-book and the dictates of a teacher. Such approaches would ideally involve the learners in decisions about what and how they learn and would require the teacher to be an organizer and guide rather than an instructor.

learning : the process of gaining knowledge about a language as a result of formal instruction by a teacher, conscious effort by the learner and the practice of selected and specific language items and structures.

lexical item : a word or group of words used in a particular utterance with a specific meaning.

lexis : another name for vocabulary.

linear syllabus : a syllabus which is organised and ordered to the principle of adding teaching points

		to each other one at a time. Most such syllabuses are also progressive syllabuses, *i.e.* learning the first teaching point helps in learning the second teaching point which helps in learning the third etc.
lingua-franca	:	a language which is used in an area to facilitate communication between speakers of different languages.
linguicism	:	the destructions of a minority language by a more powerful one.
LSP	:	language for specific purpose.
meaningful drills	:	practice exercises designed to help the learner to repeat a particular pattern or item many times but which nevertheless require the learner to make choices relating to the meaning of the sentence he produces.
meaningless drills	:	practice exercises which require no choice and therefore are almost impossible for the learner to get wrong.
medium of communication	:	speech and writing are the basic media of communication.
medium of instruction	:	the language in which subjects in an educational institution are taught.
mistakes	:	deviations from the norms of a language caused by such non-linguistic factors as carelessness, tiredness, boredom, excitement, tension etc.
modal verbs	:	verbs which add to the meaning of the main verb. They usually indicate the attitude of the speaker or writer.
monitoring	:	the process of assessing the accuracy, appropriateness and effectiveness of one's utterances. In learning a second language it is very important to achieve the right amount of monitoring. Those learners who under-monitor usually achieve

		communication without correctness and those who over-monitor produce very correct utterances.
morphology	:	the grammar of the word.
mother-tongue	:	the language first acquired (L_1), the language of which one is a native speaker.
multi-lingual	:	a person who can use many languages.
multiple choice	:	exercises and tests requiring the learners to select the correct answer from a number of possible answers.
native language	:	the language learned as a child because it is the one used in the child's environment.
native speaker	:	a person who speaks a language as his first language, *i.e.,* as the language he first learned as a child.
norms	:	standards governing the choice of language code, what to say and where to say it.
notion	:	a concept or area of meaning such as time, duration, quantity or space.
notional approach	:	an approach to language teaching which concentrates on teaching the learners how to express different aspects of the main concepts represented by the language, *i.e.* ways of referring to the future, to quality, to time, to duration, to space, to quantity etc.
notional syllabus	:	a language teaching syllabus which concentrates on teaching points which are ways of expressing different aspects of the main concepts communicated by the language.
objective test	:	a test which has a limited, predictable and definite number of possible answers and therefore only requires the markers to follow a marking key.

ostensive definition	:	a way of demonstrating the meaning of a word or group of words by getting the learners to experience the meaning through their senses.
phonic method	:	the method of teaching reading by sounding out each letter.
pragmatics	:	the study of language from the point of view of its users and of the choices they make.
presiviptivism	:	an approach to language which lays down rules of correctness.
psycholinguistics	:	the study of the relation between linguistics and psychological processes.
register	:	a variety of language defined according to its social use.
re-mediation	:	the gradual 'putting right' of a learner's false generalisation about an aspect of a language through increasing his exposure to and monitored use of that particular aspect and thus getting the learner to generalisation.
role-play activities	:	activities in which learners play parts (*e.g.,*: waiter, customer, policeman, wife etc.) and practise language appropriate to the situations they are placed in. In this way the learners often lose some of their inhibitions and are usually less frightened of making mistakes.
rules	:	(1) Statements about normal language behaviour given to learners by grammar books, text books and teachers in the hope that they will help them to produce correct English. (2) Statements about the norms of a language.

scheme of work	:	a plan of what a teacher intends to do with a particular group of learners over a particular period of time.
second language	:	any language which is learnt formally or informally after the first, often synonymous with foreign language.
semantics	:	the branch of linguistics concerned with the study of meaning.
setting	:	the location in which an interaction is taking place.
silent way	:	a method of language teaching in which the teacher remains as silent as possible and elicits responses from the learners by using charts, rods and gestures.
simulation	:	an attempt to create a 'real' situation in the classroom with a setting, a topic, participants and situational purposes.
situational composition	:	an exercise which provides the learners with information about why they are writing and who they are writing to and then requires them to produce a piece of writing designed to achieve the situational purposes specified.
situational syllabus	:	an EFL syllabus based on lists of situations the learners are likely to have to use English in.
situational teaching	:	approaches to teaching EFL which use the creation of 'real' situations in the classroom in order to exemplify particular aspects of language use and to provide meaningful opportunities for the practice and use of language items.
speech act	:	doing something through language.
speech pathology	:	the study of abnormalities in the development and use of language in children and adults.

speech therapy	:	the profession concerned with remedying speech pathologies.
standard language	:	a dialect selected and codified for official purposes including education.
stress	:	the saying of particular sounds with greater force than others.
structural approach	:	an approach to EFL teaching based on the presentation and practice of the basic structures of the language. In other words the learners are taught the grammar of the language.
structural syllabus	:	a syllabus based on a list of structures to be taught.
style	:	(1) the particular way an author expresses himself. (2) the type of expression appropriate to particular purposes and situations.
subjective test	:	a test which requires the markers to evaluate and not just to follow a mark sheet.
substitution table	:	a means of providing practice of correct structures. The learner selects from columns and then combines the elements he has chosen in order to make a sentence.
suggestopedia	:	a humanistic teaching method which tries to make the learning as relaxed and comfortable as possible and to make maximum use of the brain's capacity to combine the conscious and the unconscious for learning.
survival English	:	the English needed by overseas visitors to an English-speaking area to manage such everyday activities as buying goods, ordering meals, cashing cheques etc.
stylistics	:	the study of varieties of language including literary varieties.

syllabus	:	a document outlining the main teaching points to be taught to a particular type of group of learners in a particular institution or group of institutions.
synchronic	:	the study of a language at one point in time.
syntagmatic	:	relating to the choices a user of a language has to make in order to relate one item in an utterance to the other items already selected.
syntax	:	the grammatical arrangement of words in an utterance. Rules of syntax thus deal with permissible combinations, word orders and obligatory agreements.
synthetic	:	a synthetic approach is one which teaches items one by one and which restricts the learner to those items he has already been taught plus a new items in each lesson.
target language (TL)	:	the language the learner is trying to learn. Thus English is the target language for any overseas student learning English as a second or foreign language.
teaching points	:	particular aspects of the language selected by the teacher for presentation to a particular class of learners.
TEFL	:	teaching English as a foreign language.
text	:	a continuous 'piece' of written or spoken language.
theme	:	a particular subject used as the basis of a unit of teaching.
topic	:	(1) what is being talked about in a particular situation. (2) a particular theme used as the basis of a unit of teaching.
transfer	:	(1) the influence of one language during the acquisition of another language.

		(2) the use of skills etc. developed in association with one language while using another language.
treatment	:	deliberate language development or invention, usually known by its French name traitement, similar to language engineering.
U	:	the language usages of the socially powerful.
Universal grammar	:	the view that the aim of linguistics is to specify the unique form of human grammar.
usage	:	language performance in artificial practice situations such as drills, exercises, multiple choice tests etc.
use	:	language performance in situations which have genuine communicative purposes and are not designed just to practise particular language items and structures.
utterance	:	any complete unit of language used for communicative purpose.
vernacular	:	a language variety which is local rather than official or international.

REFERENCES

D.A. Wilkins, *Linguistics in Language Teaching.*

D.A. Wilkins, *Notional Syllabuses.*

H.H. Stern, *Fundamental Concepts of Language Teaching.*

Ronald V. White, *The ELT Curriculum Design, Innovation and Management.*

J.C. Richards and T.S. Rodgers, *Approaches and Methods in Language Teaching.*

Wilga Rivers, *Teaching Foreign Language Skills.*

H.G. Widdowson, *Teaching English as Communication.*

Pit Corder, *Introducing Applied Linguistics.*

William Littlewood, *The Communicative Syllabus : A Systemic Functional Approach to Language Teaching.*

William Littlewood , *Communicative Language Teaching.*

Michael M. Carthy, *Spoken Language and Linguistics.*

R.L. Trask, *Key Concepts in Language and Linguistics.*

R.L. Trask, *A Dictionary of Phonetics and Phonology.*

George Yule , *The Study of Language.*

Lyle F. Backman and Andrew D. Cohen, *Interfaces between Second Language Acquisition and Language Testing Research.*

Tom McArthur, *The English Language.*

Arthur Hughes, *Testing for Language Teachers.*

T.C. Baruah, *The English Teacher's Handbook.*

Keith Johnson and Keith Morrow, *Communication in the Classroom.*

Gillian Lazar, *Literature and Language Teaching.*

Allen, *Teaching English as a Second Language.*

Kamala Nanda, *Developing English Comprehension.*

John Heycraft, *An Introduction to English Language Teaching.*

Geoffrey Broughton, Christopher Brumfit, Roger Flavell, Peter Hill, Anita Pincas, ed. *Teaching English as a Foreign Language.*

Frank Smith, *To think in Language Learning and Education.*

Roger T. Bell, *An Introduction to Applied Linguistics : Approaches and Methods in Language Teaching.*

Rod Ellis, *The Study of Second Language Acquisition.*

William Littlewood, *Foreign and Second Language Learning : Language Acquisition Research and its Implication.*

William Littlewood, *Communicative Language Teaching : An Introduction.*

Peter Skelian, *A Cognitive Approach to Language Learning.*